LONGMAN
KEYSTONE

A

Reader's Companion Workbook

Anna Uhl Chamot

John De Mado

Sharroky Hollie

PEARSON
Longman

LONGMAN KEYSTONE A

Keystone A Reader's Companion Workbook

Pearson Education, 10 Bank Street, White Plains, NY 10606

Staff credits: The people who made up the *Longman Keystone* team, representing editorial, production, design, manufacturing, and marketing are John Ade, Rhea Banker, Liz Barker, Danielle Belfiore, Don Bensey, Virginia Bernard, Kenna Bourke, Anne Boynton-Trigg, Johnnie Farmer, Maryann Finocchi, Patrice Fraccio, Geraldine Geniusas, Charles Green, Henry Hild, David L. Jones, Lucille M. Kennedy, Ed Lamprich, Emily Lippincott, Tara Maceyak, Maria Pia Marrella, Linda Moser, Laurie Neaman, Sherri Pemberton, Liza Pleva, Joan Poole, Edie Pullman, Monica Rodriguez, Tania Saiz-Sousa, Chris Siley, Lynn Sobotta, Heather St. Clair, Jennifer Stem, Siobhan Sullivan, Jane Townsend, Heather Vomero, Marian Wassner, Lauren Weidenman, Matthew Williams, and Adina Zoltan.

Cover Image: Background, John Foxx/Getty Images; Inset, Stockbyte/Getty Images
Text composition: TSI Graphics
Text font: 11 pt ITC Stone Sans Std
Photos: 2 Getty Images; 6 Cosmo Condina/Stock Connection; 7 Bert Myers/Mira; 23 NASA; 35 Ara Pacis Augustae, Rome/Canali PhotoBank, Milan/SuperStock; 57 Francesco Zizola/Magnum Photos, Inc.; 64 Peter Greste/Turtle Pond Publications; 69 Peter Greste/Turtle Pond Publications; 83 Joanna B. Pinneo/Aurora; 95 Dorling Kindersley; 101 The Art Archive; 102 © KID'S GUERNICA International Committee; 105 © KID'S GUERNICA International Committee; 119 Terje Bendiksby/Agence France Presse/Getty Images; 126 NASA/Photo Researchers, Inc.; 127 Mike Dunning/Dorling Kindersley/International Automotive Design; 128 The Granger Collection, New York; 129 Trek Aerospace, Inc.; 133 Shutterstock; 143 Dr. Jurgen Scriba/Photo Researchers, Inc.
Illustrations: Tom Leonard, 5, 10
Technical art: TSI Graphics
Acknowledgements:
Excerpt from *G Is for Googol: A Math Alphabet Book* by David M. Schwartz. Copyright © 1998 by David M. Schwartz, Tricycle Press, Berkeley, CA, www.tenspeed.com. Reprinted with permission.
"Fact or Fiction?" Copyright © Pearson Longman, 10 Bank Street, White Plains, NY 10606.
"Ancient Kids." Copyright © Pearson Longman, 10 Bank Street, White Plains, NY 10606.
"Amazing Growth Facts." Adapted from *Incredible Comparisons* by Russell Ash, Dorling Kindersley.
"Extraordinary People: Serving Others." Copyright © Pearson Longman, 10 Bank Street, White Plains, NY 10606.
"Soccer: The World Sport" by Jane Schwartz. Copyright © Pearson Longman, 10 Bank Street, White Plains, NY 10606.
"Going, Going, Gone?" Adapted from *Time for Kids*, January 22, 2002. © 2002 Time for Kids. Reprinted by permission.
"Ivory-Billed Woodpeckers Make Some Noise" by Jill Egan. Adapted from *Time for Kids*, August 5, 2005. © 2005 Time for Kids. Reprinted by permission.
"Kids' Guernica." Copyright © Pearson Longman, 10 Bank Street, White Plains, NY 10606.
"A Tree Grows in Kenya: The Story of Wangari Maathai" and "How to Plant a Tree." Copyright © Pearson Longman, 10 Bank Street, White Plains, NY 10606.
"Life in the Future." Copyright © Pearson Longman, 10 Bank Street, White Plains, NY 10606.
"Genetic Fingerprints." Copyright © Pearson Longman, 10 Bank Street, White Plains, NY 10606.

ISBN-13: 978-0-13-241244-5
ISBN-10: 0-13-241244-6

PEARSON LONGMAN ON THE **WEB**

Pearsonlongman.com offers online resources for teachers and students. Access our Companion Websites, our online catalog, and our local offices around the world.

Visit us at **pearsonlongman.com**.

Printed in the United States of America
9 10 11—V011—13 12

Contents

Unit 1

Unit 2

READING 1: "Ancient Kids"

READING 4: "Amazing Growth Facts"

Contents

Unit 3

READING 2: "Extraordinary People: Serving Others"

READING 4: "Friendship and Cooperation in the Animal Kingdom"

Unit 4

READING 1: "Soccer: The World Sport"

READING 4: "Going, Going, Gone?" / "Ivory-Billed Woodpeckers Make Noise"

Contents

Unit 5

READING 2: "Kids' Guernica"

READING 4: "A Tree Grows in Kenya: The Story of Wangari Maathai" / "How to Plant a Tree"

Contents

Unit 6

READING 1: "Life in the Future"

READING 4: "Genetic Fingerprints"

Contents

Name _____ Date _____

UNIT 1 — Can all mysteries be solved?

READING 2: From *G Is for Googol*

SUMMARY   *Use with textbook pages 22–25.*

These two sections from *G Is for Googol* describe an unusual number sequence that is found in nature, art, architecture, music, and poetry. "F Is for Fibonacci" tells about the Italian mathematician named Fibonacci who discovered the mysterious number sequence in the 1200s. The first 12 numbers in the series are 1, 1, 2, 3, 5, 8, 13, 21, 34, 55, 89, and 144. When you add one number to the next, you get the following number in the sequence. "N Is for Nature" explains how to find the Fibonacci sequence in pinecones and other natural objects, including sunflower seeds, pineapples, and artichokes.

Visual Summary

```
                  ┌─────────────────────────┐
                  │      G Is for Googol     │
                  └─────────────────────────┘
                               │
          ┌────────────────────┴────────────────────┐
```

Who was Fibonacci?	**Where are Fibonacci numbers found?**
An Italian mathematician in the 1200s	Throughout nature
Wrote a book about numbers	Count the number of petals in flowers
Wanted Europeans to use Arabic numbers	Count the number of spirals in pinecones
Discovered this mysterious number sequence: 1, 1, 2, 3, on to infinity	Count the number of spirals formed by a sunflower's seeds
Add one number to the next and you get the next number in the sequence	Count the number of spirals formed by the diamond-shaped markings on a pineapple

From G Is for Googol
by David M. Schwartz

Did you know that a googol is a 1 followed by 100 zeroes? G Is for Googol is a math alphabet book that explains many unusual mathematical words and facts. Read two sections from this amazing book. Both are about a mysterious number sequence.

F Is for Fibonacci

In the 1200s, an Italian mathematician named Leonardo of Pisa wrote a book about numbers. He signed his name *Fibonacci* (pronounced fib-o-NOTCH-ee).

In his book, Fibonacci said that the people of Europe should stop using Roman numerals. He wanted everyone to switch to the numerals used in the Arabic world. Instead of writing LXXVIII, they could write 78. Isn't 78 easier to write than LXXVIII? Well, Fibonacci thought so, and because of him, we use Arabic numerals today.

Fibonacci's book also included story problems. One was about rabbits: How many pairs of rabbits will there be each month if you start with one pair of newborn rabbits, and that pair produces a pair of babies every month? The rabbits start producing babies when they are two months old, and their babies also have their first babies when they become two months old.

---

producing, having

Here's one way to look at it:

After How Long?	How Many Rabbits?
Starting point	1 pair
After 1 month	1 pair
After 2 months	2 pairs
After 3 months	3 pairs
After 4 months	5 pairs
After 5 months	8 pairs
After 6 months	13 pairs
After 7 months	21 pairs
After 8 months	34 pairs
After 9 months	55 pairs
After 10 months	89 pairs
After 11 months	144 pairs

Let's look at the answers another way:

| 1 1 2 3 5 8 13 21 34 55 89 144 |

These are the first 12 numbers in the famous *Fibonacci sequence* of numbers.

See if you can figure out what's so special about the Fibonacci sequence. After the first two numbers, how can the others be made? Think about it before you read on.

Whenever you add one number to the next, you get the following number in the sequence. Try it. Add 2 and 3. What do you get? Now add 5 and 8. Got it? Okay, now what number comes after 144 in the Fibonacci sequence?

Fibonacci numbers are interesting, but what's *amazing* about them is how often they appear. You can find Fibonacci numbers in art, architecture, music, poetry, and nature. Read **N Is for Nature**. Get ready to be amazed.

---

figure out, think about a problem or situation until you find the answer or understand what has happened

Reading Strategy: Use Visuals

Visuals can help you to better understand the information in an article. Circle the chart on this page. What does the chart show?

_____

_____

_____

Text Structure

A science text often has highlighted terms. Their definitions are at the bottom of the page. Circle the highlighted term on this page and underline its definition. Write a new sentence using the term.

_____

_____

_____

Comprehension Check

Underline the sentence that lists the different areas where you can find the Fibonacci sequence. According to the author, what is amazing about this number sequence?

_____

_____

_____

N Is for Nature

There are numbers in *nature*. Lots.

Do you remember the Fibonacci sequence of numbers? Here are the first twelve numbers of the Fibonacci sequence:

1	1	2	3	5	8	13	21	34	55	89	144

Fibonacci discovered this number sequence, but he did not invent it. Nature invented it. If each page of this book stated one way that Fibonacci numbers appear in nature, we'd need a book so heavy you couldn't lift it. Here are just a few.

The number of petals in a flower is usually a Fibonacci number. Some flowers, like daisies, don't have true petals, but petal-like parts called *florets*. Florets come in Fibonacci numbers, too.

Pine needles come in groups, or *bundles*. The bundles almost always have 1, 2, 3, or 5 needles. Do these numbers look familiar?

---

petals, the brightly colored parts of a flower

But pine needles aren't nearly as interesting as pinecones. Find a pinecone. The hard little knobby parts are called *bracts*. (Make sure your pinecone is in good condition, with no missing bracts.) Turn the cone so you're looking at its base. Can you see how the bracts make spirals? There are clockwise spirals, and there are counterclockwise spirals. Follow one spiral as it winds all the way around the cone to the pointy end. Dab a little paint on each bract in that spiral. Now dab a different color on a spiral going in the other direction. You'll see that one spiral winds gradually, and the other one winds more steeply. How many of each type are there? Count them. Remember, it's not the number of bracts that you're counting; it's the number of spirals.

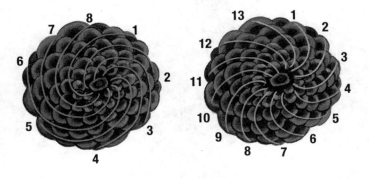

▲ If you count the clockwise or counterclockwise spirals on the bottom of a pinecone, you will get a Fibonacci number.

Text Structure

Mark the Text

Science articles often include experiments. Underline the first step and the last step in the pinecone experiment on this page. What does the author suggest you use to mark each bract in a spiral?

_____

_____

_____

Comprehension Check

Mark the Text

Underline the sentence that explains what a *bract* is. What is the relationship between a bract and a spiral?

_____

_____

_____

Reading Strategy: Use Visuals

Mark the Text

Visuals help you to better understand a text. Circle the images on this page. What do they show? How do they help you understand more about the Fibonacci sequence?

_____

_____

_____

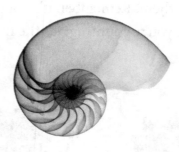

Some pinecones have 3 gradual spirals and 5 steep spirals. Some have 5 gradual and 8 steep. Or 8 and 13. Or 13 and 21. A pinecone's spirals come in Fibonacci numbers. In fact, Fibonacci numbers are sometimes called "pinecone numbers."

Fibonacci numbers could also be called "sunflower numbers," "artichoke numbers," or "pineapple numbers" because you will find the numbers in spirals formed by a sunflower's seeds, an artichoke's leaves, and a pineapple's scales (the diamond-shaped markings on the outside).

Fibonacci strikes again!

▲ These seashells have spirals that follow the Fibonacci sequence.

No one really understands why Fibonacci numbers show up so much in nature. It's a mystery!

Here's another way that Fibonacci numbers are found in nature: They make a spiral that maintains a constant proportion all the way to infinity. To find that spiral, take a rectangle that has "Fibonacci" proportions, say 3" × 5", then repeat that same proportioned rectangle, smaller and smaller . . .

---

maintains, continues in the same way
proportion, the amount of something compared to something else

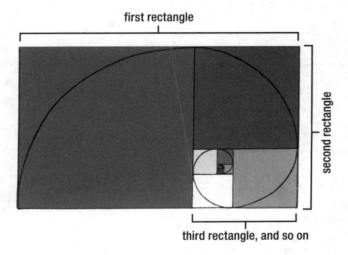

first rectangle

second rectangle

third rectangle, and so on

Choose one and complete:

1. Make a poster to show Fibonacci numbers. Explain how the sequence works.

2. Use reliable sources at the library or on the Internet to learn more about Fibonacci's findings. Write a one-page report on his work and life.

3. Make a drawing that shows how Fibonacci numbers appear in nature.

Comprehension Check

Underline the sentence that describes another way the Fibonacci numbers are found in nature. Describe how to find the spiral that keeps a constant proportion all the way to infinity.

Mark the Text

_____

_____

_____

Text Structure

Draw a box around the first highlighted word on this page. Look at the definition. Then use the word in a new sentence.

Mark the Text

_____

_____

_____

Reading Strategy: Use Visuals

Circle the diagram on this page. How does it help explain ideas in the text?

Mark the Text

_____

_____

_____

Retell It!

Write a short entry about Fibonacci for an encyclopedia. Explain who he was and what is important about the number sequence he discovered.

_____

_____

_____

_____

_____

_____

_____

_____

Reader's Response

Did the article make you think differently about the role of numbers in nature? If so, how did it change your thinking? If not, why?

_____

_____

_____

_____

Think About the Skill

How did using the visuals help you to better understand the article? Give some specific examples.

_____

_____

_____

_____

EDIT FOR MEANING

Read

You have read two sections from *G Is for Googol.* Now read one paragraph from it again.

F Is for Fibonacci

In his book, Fibonacci said that the people of Europe should stop using Roman numerals. He wanted everyone to switch to the numerals used in the Arabic world. Instead of writing LXXVIII, they could write 78. Isn't 78 easier to write than LXXVIII? Well, Fibonacci thought so, and because of him, we use Arabic numerals today.

The paragraphs below and on the next page contain the same information as the paragraph you just read. However, each contains one error. First, find the error. Then fix it by editing the sentence so that the information is correct. The first one has been done for you.

Example. Find and fix the error.

F Is for Fibonacci

In his book, Fibonacci said that the ~~rulers of Asia and Africa~~ *people of Europe* should stop using Roman numerals. According to Fibonacci, everyone should change to using the numbers used in Arabic countries. For example, instead of writing LXXVIII, people could write 78. It seemed much easier to write 78 than LXXVIII. Because of Fibonacci, we use Arabic numerals today.

Fix the Error

1. Find and fix the error.

F Is for Fibonacci

In his book, Fibonacci argued that Europeans should stop using Roman numerals. He wanted everyone to switch to using Arabic numerals. Instead of writing LXXVIII, for example, people could write 78. Isn't 78 easier to write than LXXVIII? Well, Fibonacci thought so and others agreed. Partly because of him, Roman numerals are widely used today.

2. Find and fix the error.

F Is for Fibonacci

Fibonacci argued in his book that Europeans should stop using Roman numerals. Instead, he wanted everyone to switch to the numerals used in the Arabic world. Fibonacci wanted people to write LXXVIII instead of 78. Thanks to him, we use Arabic numerals today.

FOCUS ON DETAILS

Crossword Puzzle

To complete this crossword puzzle, you'll need to remember or search for details in the reading. Use the words in the word box to help you. Not all of the words in the word box are in the puzzle. Fill in the crossword with answers to the clues below. The first answer has been done for you.

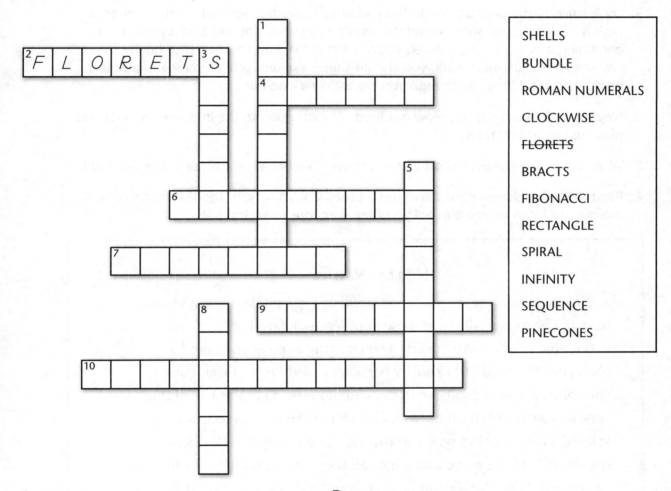

SHELLS

BUNDLE

ROMAN NUMERALS

CLOCKWISE

~~FLORETS~~

BRACTS

FIBONACCI

RECTANGLE

SPIRAL

INFINITY

SEQUENCE

PINECONES

Across

2. The petal-like parts of some flowers
4. The hard, knobby parts of pinecones
6. Rotating in the direction that a clock's hands move
7. A space or distance without limits or an end
9. A collection of numbers in a particular order
10. Numbers like LXVI, instead of 66

Down

1. A 13th-century Italian mathematician
3. A shape that goes around and around as it goes up or down
5. A four-sided shape with right angles
8. A group of pine needles

Unit 1 • Reading 2

1. Silently read the text below. Make sure you understand the point that each sentence is making.

2. Underline the word or words in each sentence that are most important. When you read, you should say these underlined words with expression.

3. Look again at the punctuation in the paragraphs. Remember that when a sentence ends in a period, you should read the words as a statement and take a breath before beginning a new sentence. When you see a comma, you should pause briefly. When you see an exclamation mark, you should sound excited. When you see a question mark, you should read as though you are asking a question.

4. Now read the paragraphs below out loud. Pay attention to the important words and punctuation as you read.

5. Write down any words that slowed you down. Practice saying these words out loud.

6. Read the text below out loud two more times. You may want to ask a friend or family member to listen to you and tell you their reactions to your reading.

N Is for Nature

Pine needles come in groups, or *bundles*. The bundles almost always have 1, 2, 3, or 5 needles. Do these numbers look familiar?

But pine needles aren't nearly as interesting as pinecones. Find a pinecone. The hard little knobby parts are called *bracts*. (Make sure your pinecone is in good condition, with no missing bracts.) Turn the cone so you're looking at its base. Can you see how the bracts make spirals? There are clockwise spirals, and there are counterclockwise spirals. Follow one spiral as it winds all the way around the cone to the pointy end. Dab a little paint on each bract in that spiral. Now dab a different color on a spiral going in the other direction. You'll see that one spiral winds gradually, and the other one winds more steeply. How many of each type are there? Count them. Remember, it's not the number of bracts that you're counting; it's the number of spirals.

Name _____ Date _____

Can all mysteries be solved?

READING 3: "Fact or Fiction?"

SUMMARY *Use with textbook pages 34–39.*

This passage explores some mysterious places, creatures, and events. First it describes three unexplained mysteries in Egypt. It tells about the design of the Great Pyramids, the age of the Great Sphinx, and the curse on Tutankhamen's tomb. Then the article asks why people abandoned the mountain-top city of Machu Picchu. It questions why people built the circle of huge rocks known as Stonehenge. And it asks why there are hundreds of large statues on Easter Island. The article also describes reports of strange creatures. These include giant octopuses and squid, the famous Loch Ness monster, and the ape-like Bigfoot and yeti.

Visual Summary

GREAT MYSTERIES from around the world	
Where?	*What?*
Egypt	The Pyramids of Giza The Great Sphinx The Curse of King Tutankhamen
Peru	The Abandoned City of Machu Picchu
England	Stonehenge
Easter Island	Giant Statues called Moai
The Ocean	Giant Sea Creatures
Scotland	The Loch Ness Monster
United States	Bigfoot or Sasquatch
Tibet	Yeti

Use What You Know

List three real life mysteries you have heard or read about.

1. _____

2. _____

3. _____

Text Structure

A social studies text often has highlighted words. Their definitions are at the bottom of the page. Circle the first highlighted word on this page and underline its definition. Reread the sentence in which it appears. Rewrite the sentence without using the highlighted term.

Mark the Text

_____

_____

_____

Reading Strategy: Preview

Good readers preview a text before they begin to read. Previewing can help you to better understand what you read. Underline the first sentence of the second paragraph. What do you think this paragraph might be about?

Mark the Text

_____

_____

_____

Fact or Fiction?

Path to the Stars?

About 4,500 years ago, the pharaoh Cheops and his son and grandson built the three Pyramids of Giza in Egypt. These pyramids were tombs, or places to bury the dead. For thousands of years, people didn't understand why these three pyramids were grouped together.

Then Belgian engineer Robert Bauval noticed that the shape of the three pyramids was the same as part of a group of stars in the sky called Orion's Belt. The whole group of stars—Orion—was sacred to the Egyptians. When Cheops died, he was buried in the Great Pyramid of Giza. The Egyptians made a shaft—or hole—in this pyramid. The shaft led from Cheops's tomb to the sky and the three stars of Orion's Belt. Scientists believe that the Egyptians built this shaft so that Cheops could fly from the pyramid to Orion. There, he would become a god.

---

pharaoh, ancient Egyptian ruler
engineer, person who plans how to build machines, roads, and so on

The Secret of the Great Sphinx

A huge statue with the head of a man and the body of a lion stands in Giza, Egypt. Known as the Great Sphinx, it seems to defend the pyramids behind it. Like the pyramids, the Sphinx is made from limestone, which is very common in Egypt. The exact age of the Sphinx remains one of the world's great mysteries. For thousands of years, wind and sand have eroded this enormous sculpture. Some archaeologists believe that water also damaged the Sphinx many centuries ago. Was the Sphinx once buried at the bottom of the sea? No one knows for sure.

Mysterious Cities

Some ancient cities were abandoned and no one knows why. One of these cities is Machu Picchu, located about 2,440 meters (8,000 ft.) high in the Andes Mountains of Peru. The Inca built Machu Picchu from about 1460 to 1470 C.E. They lived in parts of South America, including what is now Peru. They used stone blocks to make most of the buildings. The blocks fit together perfectly.

---

statue, shape of a person or animal made of stone, metal, or wood
limestone, a type of rock that contains calcium, often used to make buildings
eroded, slowly destroyed
centuries, periods of 100 years
abandoned, left completely behind and not used anymore

Reading Strategy: Preview

Circle the two headings on this page. What do you think each section might be about? **Mark the Text**

1. _____

2. _____

Comprehension Check

Circle the name of the famous statue in Giza, Egypt. What does this giant statue look like? **Mark the Text**

_____

_____

_____

Text Structure

Social studies articles often include important dates. Underline the sentence that tells when Machu Picchu was built. Where is the city located? **Mark the Text**

_____

_____

_____

Text Structure

Circle the first highlighted word on this page and underline its definition. Then use the highlighted word in a new sentence.

_____

_____

_____

Reading Strategy: Preview

Draw a box around the heading on this page. Then add some words to the heading to turn it into a question.

_____

_____

_____

Comprehension Check

Underline the sentence that tells when Stonehenge was built. Why do you think researchers don't know exactly who built this monument?

_____

_____

_____

In the early 1500s, everyone left the city. No one knows why. Perhaps people died or left because of smallpox, a deadly disease that was brought to the Americas by European explorers and colonists. Machu Picchu was forgotten for hundreds of years. Then, in 1911, the American explorer Hiram Bingham rediscovered it. Today, tourists from all over the world visit this unique city.

Stonehenge

Stonehenge is a mysterious monument of huge stones in England. Ancient peoples built Stonehenge about 5,000 years ago. No one really knows who these people were or why they built this strange circle of rocks.

Some people believe that Stonehenge was a temple to the sun. Other people believe that Stonehenge was a great stone calendar or calculator. They think that the stones were arranged to measure the sun's movements. For example, the stones may have been used to measure the summer and winter solstices—the longest and shortest days of the year. Perhaps Stonehenge was created to mark the rise of the sun and moon throughout the centuries. How will we ever know for sure?

_____

colonists, people who settle in a new country or area
monument, something that is built to help people to remember an important person or event
temple, holy building
calculator, instrument used to figure out mathematical problems

Island of Giants

Easter Island is a tiny island in the Pacific Ocean, 3,620 kilometers (2,250 mi.) off the coast of Chile. It was named by Dutch explorers who arrived there on Easter Sunday, 1722. The island is covered with nearly 900 large statues, called "moai." Scientists believe the statues are the gods of the ancient people of Easter Island—the Rapa Nui people. But no one knows for sure. Another mystery is how the Rapa Nui people moved the heavy stones as far as 23 kilometers (14 mi.).

Archaeologists have found wooden tablets with the ancient language of the Rapa Nui people on them. No one knows how to read this language today. So the history of the Rapa Nui people is still a puzzle. Only the great stone statues remain to watch over the island.

Easter Sunday, a special Sunday in March or April when Christians remember Christ's death and his return to life

Reading Strategy: Preview

Previewing can help you guess the main subject of a text. Circle the heading on this page. What do you think this section might be about?

_____

_____

_____

Text Structure

Social studies includes geography, which is the study of places around the world. Underline the sentence that tells who arrived on Easter Island in the 1700s. Where is the island located?

_____

_____

_____

Comprehension Check

Underline the sentence that tells what archaeologists have found on the island. Who were the Rapa Nui?

_____

_____

_____

Mark the Text

Curse of the Pharaoh

Tutankhamen was a pharaoh in ancient Egypt from 1333 to 1324 B.C.E. When he died, Tutankhamen was buried in a tomb with gold and other treasures.

In 1922, a group led by British archaeologists Howard Carter and Lord Carnarvon opened the tomb of Tutankhamen. They found many treasures, including a beautiful gold mask. Some people believed that a message carved in the tomb wall said, "Death will slay with his wings whoever disturbs the peace of the pharaoh." Lord Carnarvon died soon after opening the tomb. According to one story, Carnarvon's dog died at the same time at his home in England. Then, five months after Carnarvon died, his younger brother died suddenly.

According to one report, six of the twenty-six people at the opening of Tutankhamen's tomb died within ten years. However, many other people who were there when the tomb was opened lived to be very old. Was there really a curse? What do you think?

---

message, information that is communicated in words or signals
slay, kill
curse, wish that something bad would happen to someone

Terrifying Tentacles

Scientists say that we know more about Mars than we do about the mysteries at the bottom of the ocean. For instance, little is known about giant octopuses and squid. These sea creatures are usually only about 60 to 90 centimeters (2–3 ft.) long. However, there have been reports of giant octopuses and squid with tentacles long enough to pull a ship underwater. In 1753, a man in Norway described a huge sea monster "full of arms." The man said that the monster looked big enough to crush a large ship. More recently, giant squid have been discovered with tentacles 10 meters (33 ft.) long. Imagine eating calamari rings the size of truck tires!

Scary Monsters

Most people believe that dinosaurs disappeared millions of years ago. However, a few dinosaurs may have survived. The famous Loch Ness monster may be a living dinosaur-like reptile called a plesiosaur.

---

tentacles, long, thin arm-like parts
calamari rings, sliced squid, often served fried or in a salad
reptile, type of animal, such as a snake or lizard, whose
　　blood changes temperature according to the temperature
　　around it

Comprehension Check

Underline the sentence that compares our understanding of Mars to what we know about the bottom of the ocean. Why do you think scientists don't know very much about the bottom of the ocean?

_____

_____

_____

Text Structure

Circle the first highlighted term on this page. Look at its definition. Then use the word in a new sentence.

_____

_____

_____

Comprehension Check

Circle the sentence that tells what the Loch Ness Monster might be. How long ago did dinosaurs disappear?

_____

People first reported seeing the Loch Ness monster in April 1933 when a new road was built on the north shore of Loch Ness, a lake in Scotland. A man and woman saw a huge creature with two black humps swimming across the lake. Then two more people saw a strange animal crossing the road with a sheep in its mouth. There is now a Loch Ness Investigation Bureau, but most scientists believe that the Loch Ness monster is a creature of fantasy.

Bigfoot and the Yeti

In various parts of the world, people have told stories about seeing large ape-like creatures. Different cultures give the creature different names. In the United States, for example, this creature is called Bigfoot or Sasquatch. In Tibet, it is called the yeti.

---

humps, raised parts on the back of an animal
various, different

The first reports of Bigfoot date back to 1811. At that time, a man reported seeing footprints 36 centimeters (14 in.) long. In 1924, another man claimed that Bigfoot had kidnapped him. Each year many people in the United States claim to see Bigfoot. They often report seeing the creature in the forests of the Northwest.

Reports of a huge creature frightened the first European travelers in Tibet. (In Tibet, the word *yeti* means "man-like creature.") In 1951, a Mount Everest explorer found giant footprints in the snow.

Do creatures like the yeti and Bigfoot really exist, or are they figments of the imagination? Bernard Heuvelmans (1916–2001), a famous zoologist, believed that the world is full of creatures still unknown to science. What do you think?

---

figments of the imagination, things imagined to be real that do not exist
zoologist, scientist who studies animals

Reading Strategy: Preview

Remember that you should preview a text before you begin to read. Underline the first sentence on this page. What do you think this section will be about?

_____

_____

_____

Text Structure

Social studies articles often define or explain key terms within the text. Circle the definition of *yeti*. Use this definition to describe what the yeti's footprints probably looked like.

_____

_____

_____

_____

Comprehension Check

Underline the sentence that tells who Bernard Heuvelmans was. What do you think he would say about the existence of Bigfoot?

_____

_____

_____

Choose one and complete:

1. Draw a picture showing what one of the mystery creatures described in the text might look like.

2. Use reliable sources at the library or on the Internet to find out about another great mystery. Write a one-page report on what you find.

3. Work with a group of classmates to write and perform a short play about researchers working to solve one of the mysteries discussed in the reading.

Retell It!

Choose four mysteries from the reading. Write a riddle about each one. Here's an example: I am a mysterious monument of stones in England. What am I? *(Stonehenge)*

_____

_____

_____

_____

_____

_____

_____

Reader's Response

What mystery did you find the most interesting? Why?

_____

_____

_____

_____

_____

Think About the Skill

How did previewing help you to better understand the article?

_____

_____

_____

_____

EDIT FOR MEANING

Read

You have read "Fact or Fiction?" Now read one paragraph from it again.

Island of Giants

Archaeologists have found wooden tablets with the ancient language of the Rapa Nui people on them. No one knows how to read this language today. So the history of the Rapa Nui people is still a puzzle. Only the great stone statues remain to watch over the island.

Fix the Error

Each paragraph below contains the same information as the paragraph you just read. However, each paragraph contains one error. First, find the error. Then fix it by editing the sentence so that the information is correct.

1. Find and fix the error.

Island of Giants

Today, Easter Island is bare except for the giant statues that stare out over the island. Archaeologists know little about the history of the Rapa Nui people. They have found wooden tablets written in the ancient language of the Rapa Nui. Many people still speak this language today.

---

2. Find and fix the error.

Island of Giants

The history of the Rapa Nui people is well known to scientists. Archaeologists have found pieces of wood with the ancient language of the Rapa Nui people written on them, but no one understands this language. Now, Easter Island is quiet. Only the huge stone statues stand guard on the island.

Name _____ Date _____

FOCUS on DETAILS

Word Search Puzzle

To complete this word search puzzle, you'll need to remember or search for details in the reading. Look at the clues and circle the answers in the puzzle. Check off each clue after you've found the answer. Write each word next to its clue.

1. ☑ Ancient tombs built in Egypt _____ *pyramids* _____
2. ☐ Huge statue with the head of a man and the body of a lion _____
3. ☐ City in Peru that was abandoned in the early 1500s _____
4. ☐ Stone monument in England _____
5. ☐ Small island with giant carved statues _____
6. ☐ Pharaoh whose tomb may have been cursed _____
7. ☐ Real creature with tentacles 10 meters long _____
8. ☐ Possible dinosaur-like reptile in Scotland _____
9. ☐ Apelike creature from Tibet _____
10. ☐ Another name for Bigfoot in the United States _____

```
K  I  M  A  C  H  U  P  I  C  C  H  U  O  R
T  E  T  I  H  V  H  E  I  I  D  M  S  E  G
H  V  J  U  T  D  O  R  B  J  S  D  T  D  I
C  X  M  A  T  C  D  I  C  C  S  S  N  I  A
S  A  S  Q  U  A  T  C  H  N  N  P  Q  U  N
L  G  Y  B  Y  L  N  E  S  O  R  H  L  A  T
X  N  L  O  P  L  P  K  M  M  U  I  Q  W  S
P  Y  R  A  M  I  D  S  H  L  C  N  K  T  Q
A  N  L  Z  N  R  S  J  D  A  Q  X  T  T  U
D  K  V  N  B  E  J  B  B  B  M  O  D  X  I
N  I  H  X  N  T  K  P  L  N  Y  E  T  I  D
N  O  X  H  D  S  T  O  N  E  H  E  N  G  E
Q  F  C  H  X  B  Y  U  D  Q  Z  D  I  X  A
S  O  L  W  J  E  J  P  K  Z  T  B  R  P  H
L  E  A  S  T  E  R  I  S  L  A  N  D  N  X
```

Unit 1 • Reading 3   **25**

1. Silently read the text below. Make sure you understand the point that each sentence is making.

2. Underline the word or words in each sentence that are most important. When you read, you should say these underlined words with expression.

3. Look again at the punctuation in the paragraphs. Remember that when a sentence ends in a period, you should read the words as a statement and take a breath before beginning a new sentence. When you see a comma, you should pause briefly. When you see an exclamation mark, you should sound excited. When you see a question mark, you should read as though you are asking a question.

4. Now read the paragraphs below out loud. Pay attention to the important words and punctuation as you read.

5. Write down any words that slowed you down. Practice saying these words out loud.

6. Read the text below out loud two more times. You may want to ask a friend or family member to listen to you and tell you their reactions to your reading.

Terrifying Tentacles

Scientists say that we know more about Mars than we do about the mysteries at the bottom of the ocean. For instance, little is known about giant octopuses and squid. These sea creatures are usually only about 60 to 90 centimeters (2–3 ft.) long. However, there have been reports of giant octopuses and squid with tentacles long enough to pull a ship underwater. In 1753, a man in Norway described a huge sea monster "full of arms." The man said that the monster looked big enough to crush a large ship. More recently, giant squid have been discovered with tentacles 10 meters (33 ft.) long. Imagine eating calamari rings the size of truck tires!

UNIT 2

How does growing up change us?

READING 1: "Ancient Kids"

SUMMARY *Use with textbook pages 74–79.*

This passage tells what it was like to be a child in ancient Greek, Roman, and Maya cultures. It describes what happened when babies were born. It tells how boys and girls were raised differently. It also tells about education. In Greece, only boys went to school. In Rome, rich boys and girls went to school, but the boys stayed in school longer. In Maya culture, school was free. Both boys and girls went to school. In all these cultures, children played with toys and had pets. Some toys, games, and pets were the same from one culture to the next. Others were quite different.

Visual Summary

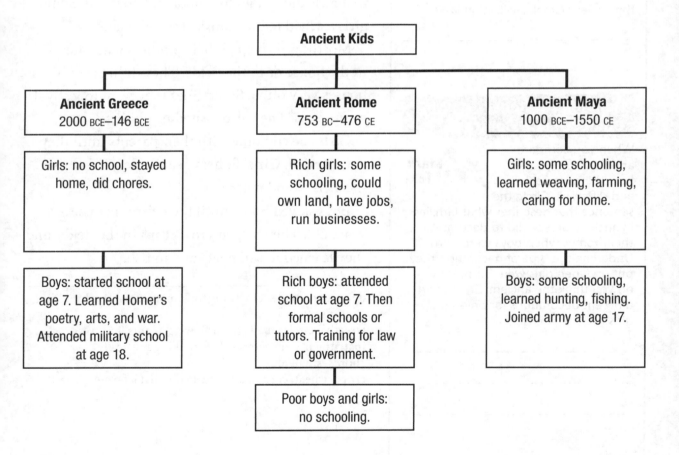

Use What You Know

List three facts you know about the ancient Greeks, Romans, and Maya.

1. _____
2. _____
3. _____

Text Structure

Social studies articles often include timelines, which show important dates in history.
Locate the timeline on this page. On the timeline, draw boxes around the beginning and ending dates for ancient Greece. About how long did the ancient Greek civilization last?

Mark the Text

_____

_____

Reading Strategy: Compare and Contrast

When you compare and contrast, you tell how things are alike and different. Circle the sentence that describes what families in ancient Greece did to decorate their homes when boys were born. Underline the type of decoration they put up when girls were born. Why do you think the ancient Greeks had different decorations for boys and girls?

Mark the Text

_____

_____

_____

Ancient Kids

Growing Up in Ancient Greece

ANCIENT GREECE

| 2000 B.C.E. | 146 B.C.E. 0 | 2000 C.E. |

When a baby was born in ancient Greece, the father performed a ritual. He did a dance, holding the newborn baby. For boy babies, the family decorated the house with wreaths of olives. For girl babies, the family decorated the house with wreaths made of wool.

There were many differences in the lives of boys and girls as they grew up. One main difference was that girls did not go to school and boys did. Some girls learned to play musical instruments.

Mostly, girls helped their mothers with chores in the house or in the fields. They didn't leave their houses very often. Sometimes they went to festivals or funerals. They also visited neighbors.

Girls stayed home with their parents until they got married. Girls' fathers usually decided whom the girls would marry.

Boys stayed home until they were six or seven years old. They helped grow crops in the fields, and they learned to sail boats and to fish.

---

decorated, made something look more attractive by adding things to it
wreaths, circles made from flowers, plants, or leaves
instruments, objects used for making music
chores, small jobs
crops, wheat, corn, fruit, and so on, that a farmer grows

When boys were about seven years old, they started their formal education. They went to school and learned reading, writing, and mathematics. They had to memorize everything because there were no school books! They memorized the poetry of Homer, a famous poet. They also learned to play a musical instrument, such as the lyre.

At school, boys learned about the arts and war. They also learned how to be good citizens. At the age of eighteen, boys went to military school for two years.

Children played with many toys, such as rattles, clay animals, pull-toys on four wheels, yo-yos, and terra-cotta dolls. Children also had pets, such as birds, dogs, goats, tortoises, and mice.

Growing Up in Ancient Rome

ANCIENT ROME

| 753 B.C.E. | 0 | 476 C.E. | 2000 C.E. |

ANCIENT GREECE

| 2000 B.C.E. | 146 B.C.E. | 0 | 2000 C.E. |

When a Roman baby was born, a relative put the baby at the feet of the father. The father picked up the baby to accept it into the family. The baby was named nine days after birth.

---

formal education, education in a subject or skill that you get in school rather than by practical experience
lyre, an ancient instrument, similar to a guitar
military school, school where students learn to fight in wars
terra-cotta, baked red clay
tortoises, land animals that move very slowly, with a hard shell covering their bodies

Reading Strategy: Compare and Contrast

Circle how old ancient Greek boys were when they started school. List three differences between what students did in school then and what students do in school now.

1. _____

2. _____

3. _____

Comprehension Check

Underline what boys did when they turned 18. Why do you think that this was necessary?

_____

_____

_____

Text Structure

Circle the two bars on the timeline. Which lasted longer—the ancient Greek or the ancient Roman culture? How do you know?

_____

_____

_____

The oldest man in a family—the father, the grandfather, or an uncle—was the "head of the family." However, women were also important to family life. They managed the house and household finances. In the early years of ancient Rome, women did not have many rights. In later years, they had more rights. They were allowed to own land and to have some types of jobs. They could manage some businesses, but they were still not allowed to hold jobs in the government or to become lawyers or teachers.

Girls and boys wore a special locket, called a *bulla*, around their necks. The bulla protected them from evil. A girl wore the bulla until her wedding day. A boy wore the bulla until he became a citizen. A boy became a citizen at age sixteen or seventeen. The family had a big celebration on this day.

Some Greeks lived in southern Italy and Sicily. The ancient Greeks had a cultural influence on the Romans. Greek teachers introduced the Romans to the Greek gods and goddesses and to Greek literature and philosophy.

School was not free. Most children in ancient Rome were not from rich families. They were poor. In poor families, parents taught their children at home. Many poor children did not learn to read or write.

---

head of the family, person who is in charge of the family
managed, controlled or directed
finances, money matters
locket, piece of jewelry like a small round box in which you put a picture of someone
influence, effect

Rich families sent their children to school at age seven to learn basic subjects. Girls did not continue in school after they learned the basic subjects. They stayed at home, where their mothers taught them how to be good wives and mothers.

Boys from rich families continued their education in formal schools or with tutors. They became lawyers or worked in government.

What did children do after school? They played with friends, pets, or toys. Toys included balls, hobbyhorses, kites, models of people and animals, hoops, stilts, marbles, and knucklebones. War games were popular with boys. Girls played with dolls. They also played board games, tic-tac-toe, and ball games.

What kind of pets did children play with in ancient Rome? Dogs were the favorite pets. Roman children also kept birds—pigeons, ducks, quail, and geese—as pets. Some children even had pet monkeys.

---

tutors, teachers of one student or a small group of students
models, small copies
stilts, a pair of poles you can stand on, used for walking high above the ground
quail, small fat birds that are hunted and shot for food and sport

---

Reading Strategy: Compare and Contrast

Circle the age at which rich Roman children went to school. What is the difference between how girls and boys were educated?

Mark the Text

_____

_____

_____

Text Structure

Draw a box around the second highlighted word on this page. Look at its definition. Then use the word in a new sentence.

Mark the Text

_____

_____

_____

Comprehension Check

Underline the favorite pet of children in ancient Rome. Then name three Roman pets that are not so common today.

Mark the Text

1. _____

2. _____

3. _____

Text Structure

Social studies includes geography, the study of places around the world. Circle the names of countries where the ancient Maya once lived. How do we know that they built cities there long ago?

_____

_____

_____

Reading Strategy: Compare and Contrast

Compare and contrast the roles of men and women in ancient Maya society. What was one difference in their roles?

_____

_____

_____

Comprehension Check

Underline what happened to an ancient Maya boy when he was five years old. Then circle two more things young men did before they married. What is one tradition a modern-day culture has for young men today?

_____

_____

_____

Growing Up in the Ancient Maya Culture

ANCIENT MAYA

1000 B.C.E.　　　0　　　1550 C.E.　2000 C.E.

ANCIENT ROME

753 B.C.E.　　0　476 C.E.　　　　2000 C.E.

ANCIENT GREECE

2000 B.C.E.　　146 B.C.E.　0　　　　2000 C.E.

The Maya lived throughout parts of southern Mexico and Central America, including Belize and Guatemala. They built large cities and created extraordinary art and architecture. You can visit the ruins of some ancient Maya cities, such as Chichén Itzá in Mexico's Yucatan region.

In Maya culture, the father was the head of the family. Maya men worked hard to support their families, and they paid taxes to the government. Women in Maya society cooked, made cloth, sewed clothing, and took care of the children.

When a boy was about five years old, the Maya tied a small white bead to the top of his head. When a girl was about five, the Maya tied a red shell around her waist. When boys and girls were twelve or thirteen years old, the village had a big ceremony that marked the end of childhood. During the ceremony, a priest cut the beads from the boys' heads. Mothers removed the red shells from the girls' waists. After the ceremony, boys and girls could get married. Young men painted themselves black until they were married.

---

ruins, the parts of buildings that are left after other parts have been destroyed
taxes, money that must be given

Maya boys and girls, unlike Roman children, did not have to pay to go to school. They learned from their parents, too. Girls learned how to weave and cook. Boys learned to hunt and fish. Children also learned how to grow crops, such as corn. At age seventeen, boys joined the army to learn about war and fighting.

Children played games and they played with toys. Some of their toys had wheels. Surprisingly, the Maya did not use wheels in their work or transportation. However, toys, such as animal pull-toys, had wheels.

Animals were important in everyday life and religion. The Maya used animals in their art. They decorated various items with pictures of foxes, owls, jaguars, hummingbirds, eagles, and other animals. The Maya sometimes ate dogs, but they mainly used dogs for hunting. The Maya thought that dogs could guide people on the journey to the afterlife. This is why they buried dogs with their owners.

---

jaguars, large wild cats with black spots
guide, show the way to
afterlife, the life that some people believe you have after death

---

Reading Strategy: Compare and Contrast

Circle the sentence that tells one way Maya children were different from Roman children. **Mark the Text**
What is one way they were the same?

_____

_____

_____

Comprehension Check

Underline the sentence that names some animals the Maya included in their art. **Mark the Text**
Why might animals have been so important to the Maya?

_____

_____

_____

Text Structure

Draw a box around the second highlighted word on this page. **Mark the Text**
Look at its definition.
Then use the word in a new sentence.

_____

_____

_____

Choose one and complete:

1. Write a short play about the daily life of a boy or girl in one of the ancient cultures in this article. You can use resources such as the Internet or encyclopedias to find more details for your play.

2. Look at the timelines in this article. Then create a single timeline that shows when the ancient Greek, Roman, and Maya cultures all lived.

3. Create a poster about the cultures of the ancient Greeks, Romans, or Maya. Include details about the lives of these ancient people.

Retell It!

Write a letter from a child in one of the ancient cultures in this article to a friend living in a different culture. Explain what your daily life is like and how it is different from your friend's life.

_____

_____

_____

_____

_____

_____

_____

Reader's Response

Which of the three cultures was the most interesting to you? Why do you find that culture the most interesting?

_____

_____

_____

_____

_____

Think About the Skill

How did comparing and contrasting help you to better understand this article?

_____

_____

_____

_____

EDIT FOR MEANING

Read

You have read "Ancient Kids." Now read one paragraph from it again.

Growing Up in Ancient Rome

The oldest man in a family—the father, the grandfather, or an uncle—was the "head of the family." However, women were also important to family life. They managed the house and household finances. In the early years of ancient Rome, women did not have many rights. In later years, they had more rights. They were allowed to own land and to have some types of jobs. They could manage some businesses, but they were still not allowed to hold jobs in the government or to become lawyers or teachers.

Fix the Error

Each paragraph below contains the same information as the paragraph you just read. However, each paragraph contains one error. First, find the error. Then fix it by editing the sentence so that the information is correct.

1. Find and fix the error.

Growing Up in Ancient Rome

A family's oldest man was the "head of the family." It could be a father, grandfather, or uncle. Women were also important to family life. They managed the house and the household money. In the early years of ancient Rome, women had many rights. They could own land and work at jobs. They could even manage their own businesses, but they could not hold jobs in the government, law, or teaching.

---

2. Find and fix the error.

Growing Up in Ancient Rome

The "head of the family" was the oldest man in the family—father, grandfather, or uncle. Women were also valuable family members. They managed the house and its finances. In early Rome, women had few rights, but later that changed. They were allowed to own their own land and could work outside the home. They could manage some businesses and become teachers, but they could not work in the government or become lawyers.

FOCUS ON DETAILS

Word Search Puzzle

To complete this word search puzzle, you'll need to remember or search for details in the reading. Look at the clues and circle the answers in the puzzle below. Check off each clue after you've found the answer. Write each word next to its clue.

1. ☑ When boys were born, ancient Greeks put up wreaths made of these __olives__

2. ☐ The name of a famous Greek poet _____

3. ☐ Something that Greek students had to do to learn in school _____

4. ☐ Culture that influenced Rome _____

5. ☐ What a Roman boy became at 16 or 17 _____

6. ☐ A Roman locket worn by boys and girls _____

7. ☐ A job for rich Romans _____

8. ☐ Animal pull-toys in ancient Maya had these _____

9. ☐ Maya girls learned to do this _____

10. ☐ A country where the Maya culture existed _____

J	S	E	W	B	V	O	M	V	E	U	I	L	A	P
B	P	F	F	M	U	G	F	V	T	E	H	A	Y	L
C	R	M	K	E	D	L	O	T	A	I	C	W	M	O
S	O	L	E	Q	B	J	L	L	R	L	K	Y	D	L
A	H	R	A	M	J	Y	A	A	S	K	J	E	K	I
G	R	E	E	K	O	M	A	N	L	S	P	R	Q	V
Z	L	T	J	W	E	R	A	N	C	K	U	I	K	E
D	Y	F	Q	T	W	P	I	B	B	Y	A	D	M	S
Z	G	A	A	X	Q	E	T	Z	W	T	G	N	Z	N
Z	M	U	U	C	L	W	A	N	E	N	U	G	G	R
X	G	Y	C	K	U	T	Q	V	B	I	Y	Y	E	E
V	F	U	E	X	N	H	K	G	E	Z	S	M	A	R
C	I	T	I	Z	E	N	C	K	Y	X	O	H	U	Y
H	Q	G	T	Y	H	Q	T	P	O	H	G	N	M	L
V	Y	I	W	H	E	E	L	S	B	K	J	G	I	D

READ FOR FLUENCY

1. Silently read the text below. Make sure you understand the point that each sentence is making.

2. Underline the word or words in each sentence that are most important. When you read, you should say these underlined words with expression.

3. Look again at the punctuation in the paragraphs. Remember that when a sentence ends in a period, you should read the words as a statement and take a breath before beginning a new sentence. When you see a comma, you should pause briefly. When you see an exclamation mark, you should sound excited. When you see a question mark, you should read as though you are asking a question.

4. Now read the paragraphs below out loud. Pay attention to the important words and punctuation as you read.

5. Write down any words that slowed you down. Practice saying these words out loud.

6. Read the text below out loud two more times. You may want to ask a friend or family member to listen to you and tell you their reactions to your reading.

Growing Up in Ancient Rome

What did children do after school? They played with friends, pets, or toys. Toys included balls, hobbyhorses, kites, models of people and animals, hoops, stilts, marbles, and knucklebones. War games were popular with boys. Girls played with dolls. They also played board games, tic-tac-toe, and ball games.

What kind of pets did children play with in ancient Rome? Dogs were the favorite pets. Roman children also kept birds—pigeons, ducks, quail, and geese—as pets. Some children even had pet monkeys.

Name _____ Date _____

UNIT 2

How does growing up change us?

READING 4: "Amazing Growth Facts"

SUMMARY *Use with textbook pages 116–117.*

"Amazing Growth Facts" tells interesting facts about how living things grow. People
and different kinds of plants and animals grow at different rates. Some things, such as
bamboo, kelp, kangaroos, and crocodiles, grow very quickly. Others, such as clams, grow
very slowly.

Visual Summary

AMAZING GROWTH FACTS		
Facts About Plants	**Facts About Animals**	**Facts About People**
A tiny acorn grows into an enormous oak tree.	Adult kangaroos weigh 30,000 times more than baby kangaroos.	The average human baby is 50 cm long and weighs 3.4 kilos.
Bamboo can grow to the height of a three-year-old child in one day.	Eggs of golden eagles and Nile crocodiles are the same size, but adult crocodiles are much larger than adult eagles.	On average, adults grow to be 3.4 times longer and 21 times heavier than they were as babies.
Pacific kelp grows to 60 m, compared to people who grow to about 1.75 m.	Deep-sea clams take 100 years to grow as large as a fingernail.	Each person eats enough food in his or her lifetime to equal the weight of 6 elephants.

Use What You Know

List three ways people change as they grow from infants to adults.

1. _____

2. _____

3. _____

Text Structure

A science article often has highlighted words. Their definitions are at the bottom of the page. Draw a box around the highlighted word on this page. Look at its definition. Reread the sentence in which the word appears. Then rewrite the sentence without using the word.

Mark the Text

_____

_____

_____

Reading Strategy: Use Visuals

Visuals can help readers to better understand an article. Look at the diagram on this page. Circle how tall Pacific kelp grows. What can you understand about the average man compared to the two plants shown in the visual?

Mark the Text

_____

_____

_____

Amazing Growth Facts

It is one of the wonders of nature that all living things increase in size. Think about how a tiny acorn can grow into an enormous oak tree. Growth occurs at different rates. Sometimes growth is very fast. Other times it is very slow.

The average newborn baby is 50 centimeters long and weighs 3.4 kilograms. When the baby grows up and becomes an adult, he or she increases on average to 3.4 times that length and 21 times that weight. Girls and boys are about the same height and weight until early adulthood. Then boys usually grow taller and weigh more than girls.

Bamboo can grow 90 centimeters in one day—the height of an average three-year-old child. Pacific giant kelp (a kind of seaweed) can grow as much as 45 centimeters in one day.

increase, become bigger

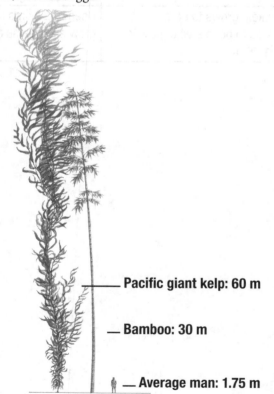

— **Pacific giant kelp: 60 m**

— **Bamboo: 30 m**

— **Average man: 1.75 m**

An ant can lift more than 100 times its weight. One hundred times the weight of a 64-kilogram person would be the same weight as three cars!

A baby kangaroo is the size and weight of a paper clip (1 gram). An adult kangaroo is 30,000 times heavier (30 kilograms). If a human grew at this rate, a 3.4-kilogram baby would weigh 102,000 kilograms as an adult—that's as much as a large whale! An average man weighs about 80 kilograms.

The egg of a golden eagle and the egg of a Nile crocodile are both 8 centimeters long. But look how much bigger the crocodile grows!

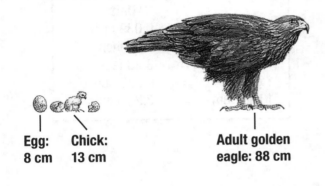

Egg: **Chick:** **Adult golden**
8 cm **13 cm** **eagle: 88 cm**

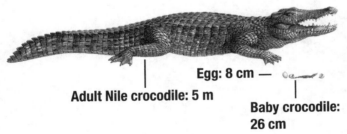

Egg: 8 cm —
Adult Nile crocodile: 5 m
Baby crocodile:
26 cm

Comprehension Check

Underline how much weight an ant can lift. How do you think our lives would be different if humans could lift that much?

_____

_____

_____

Text Structure

Science articles often present information with comparisons and contrasts to help readers understand similarities and differences. Circle the sentence that compares 1 gram to an object. List three other objects that weigh about 1 gram.

1. _____

2. _____

3. _____

Reading Strategy: Use Visuals

Visuals can present information in a different way. Look at the diagram. Draw boxes around the sizes of the golden eagle and Nile crocodile eggs. How do eagle chicks and baby crocodiles compare in size?

_____

_____

_____

A 26-centimeter baby crocodile can grow into a 5-meter adult crocodile. If humans grew at the same rate as Nile crocodiles, a 50-centimeter baby would grow into a 9.5-meter adult—more than 5 times as tall as the average person!

Clams are among the longest living and slowest growing of all creatures. A deep-sea clam takes 100 years to grow 8 millimeters. That's as big as your fingernail!

Conversion Chart		
Metric		**U.S. Customary Units**
1 millimeter	=	0.039 inch
1 centimeter	=	0.39 inch
1 meter	=	3.28 feet
1 gram	=	0.035 ounce
1 kilogram	=	2.2 pounds

In the average human life of 70 years, a heart pumps enough blood around the body to fill the fuel tanks of 700 jumbo jets. The food that we eat in our lifetime is equal in weight to the weight of six elephants! A horse's intestines are about 27 meters long. A human's intestines are about 7.5 meters long. Luckily, the intestines are curled up inside the body. Otherwise, people and horses would look very strange!

jumbo jets, very large airplanes
intestines, tubes that take food from the stomach out of the body

Intestines

Text Structure

Draw a box around the first highlighted term in the first paragraph on this page. Look at the definition. Then use the term in a new sentence.

_____

_____

_____

Comprehension Check

Underline the sentence that explains how much food a person eats in a lifetime. Did that comparison surprise you? Why or why not?

_____

_____

_____

Reading Strategy: Use Visuals

Circle the length of horse intestines and the length of human intestines. How does the diagram help you see the difference between the length of human and horse intestines?

_____

_____

_____

Choose one and complete:

1. Do research to learn more facts about growth. Make a list of the most amazing growth facts you find.

2. Use the information in this article to create your own children's book of amazing growth facts.

3. Create a skit demonstrating some of the facts in this article. You can use props such as string to show height or length.

Retell It!

Imagine you are writing a description of a TV nature show based on this article. What would you write to get viewers to tune in to the *Amazing Growth Facts* TV show?

_____

_____

_____

_____

_____

_____

_____

Reader's Response

Which fact in this article did you find the most strange and surprising? What is it about this fact that made you feel this way?

_____

_____

_____

_____

_____

Think About the Skill

How did using visuals help you better understand the article?

_____

_____

_____

_____

EDIT FOR MEANING

Read

You have read "Amazing Growth Facts." Now read one paragraph from it again.

Amazing Growth Facts

The average newborn baby is 50 centimeters long and weighs 3.4 kilograms. When the baby grows up and becomes an adult, he or she increases on average to 3.4 times that length and 21 times that weight. Girls and boys are about the same height and weight until early adulthood. Then boys usually grow taller and weigh more than girls.

Fix the Error

Each paragraph below contains the same information as the paragraph you just read. However, each paragraph contains one error. First, find the error. Then fix it by editing the sentence so that the information is correct.

1. Find and fix the error.

Amazing Growth Facts

The average newborn baby weighs 3.4 kilograms and is about 50 centimeters long. As the baby grows, he or she increases to 3.4 times that length. When the baby becomes an adult, his or her weight has decreased to about 21 times a baby's weight at birth. As children, girls and boys are about the same in size. That changes when they reach early adulthood. Then boys usually grow taller and weigh more than girls.

---

2. Find and fix the error.

Amazing Growth Facts

The average newborn baby is 50 centimeters long. Average newborns also weigh about 3.4 kilograms. When the baby becomes older, he or she grows to about 3.4 times that length. As an adult, he or she also weighs 21 times as much as a newborn. Girls and boys are about the same height, but they weigh different amounts until early adulthood. At that time, boys usually grow taller and weigh more than girls.

FOCUS ON DETAILS

Crossword Puzzle

To complete this crossword puzzle, you'll need to remember or search for details in the reading. Use the words in the word box. Not all of the words in the word box are in the puzzle. Fill in the crossword with answers to the clues below.

ACORN

CROCODILE

KANGAROO

ANT

ELEPHANTS

KELP

INCREASE

INTESTINES

KILOGRAM

~~CLAM~~

JETS

NILE

Across

2. This sea creature takes 100 years to grow

4. An enormous oak tree grows from this

6. The amount of food a human eats in a lifetime equals six of these

8. This animal is the size of a paper clip when it's born

10. To get bigger

Down

1. A measure of weight equal to 2.2 pounds

3. Long tubes that curl up inside of bodies

5. A kind of fast-growing seaweed

7. An insect that can lift 100 times its weight

9. Fast airplanes

READ FOR FLUENCY

1. Silently read the text below. Make sure you understand the point that each sentence is making.

2. Underline the word or words in each sentence that are most important. When you read, you should say these underlined words with expression.

3. Look again at the punctuation in the paragraphs. Remember that when a sentence ends in a period, you should read the words as a statement and take a breath before beginning a new sentence. When you see a comma, you should pause briefly. When you see an exclamation mark, you should sound excited. When you see a question mark, you should read as though you are asking a question.

4. Now read the paragraphs below out loud. Pay attention to the important words and punctuation as you read.

5. Write down any words that slowed you down. Practice saying these words out loud.

6. Read the text below out loud two more times. You may want to ask a friend or family member to listen to you and tell you their reactions to your reading.

Amazing Growth Facts

Clams are among the longest living and slowest growing of all creatures. A deep-sea clam takes 100 years to grow 8 millimeters. That's as big as your fingernail!

In the average human life of 70 years, a heart pumps enough blood around the body to fill the fuel tanks of 700 jumbo jets. The food that we eat in our lifetime is equal in weight to the weight of six elephants! A horse's intestines are about 27 meters long. A human's intestines are about 7.5 meters long. Luckily, the intestines are curled up inside the body. Otherwise, people and horses would look very strange!

Name _____ Date _____

UNIT
3

How does helping others help us all?

READING 2: "Extraordinary People: Serving Others"

SUMMARY *Use with textbook pages 154–157.*

This passage tells about heroes who have helped change the world. Benito Juárez became the first native Indian president of Mexico. He made Mexico a fairer, more modern country. During the Crimean War, Florence Nightingale went to Turkey with nurses from her hospital. She helped many sick and wounded soldiers. Mohandas Gandhi's ideas about nonviolent protest have influenced many. Helen Keller was blind and deaf but she learned to communicate. American president Franklin Delano Roosevelt had the disease polio. However, he helped his country during the Great Depression and World War II. Doctors Without Borders is a volunteer organization. It won the Nobel Peace Prize for helping victims of war, disease, and natural disasters.

Visual Summary

Benito Juárez	Improved education in Mexico so that every child could go to school. Made Mexico more fair and modern.
Florence Nightingale	Helped wounded soldiers and started a school for nurses.
Mohandas Gandhi	Helped achieve independence in India. Demonstrated how nonviolent protest could be used to bring about change.
Franklin Delano Roosevelt	Created jobs for people during the Great Depression. Helped the United States and the Allies win World War II.
Helen Keller	Learned to communicate even though she was blind and deaf. Inspired people not to give up when things are difficult.
Doctors Without Borders	Provides medical help to victims of war, disease, and natural disasters.

Extraordinary People: Serving Others

In different places and at different times, people have achieved extraordinary things. In the short biographies that follow, you will read about people from different times in history who helped others in many ways. You will also read about a group of people who continue to do extraordinary things in troubled parts of the world today.

Benito Juárez

Benito Juárez (1806–1872) is a national hero in Mexico. He was the son of poor Zapotec Indian farmers in the state of Oaxaca, Mexico. At age thirteen he couldn't read, write, or speak Spanish. He trained to become a priest, but later he decided to become a lawyer. As a young man, he became interested in social justice, especially the rights of native peoples. He was very popular among the native Indian population. In 1847, he was elected governor of Oaxaca.

In 1861, Juárez became the first Zapotec Indian president of Mexico. He improved education. For the first time, it was possible for every child to go to school. He stopped the French from colonizing Mexico. His many reforms made Mexico a fairer, more modern society.

---

social justice, fairness for all people
colonizing, controlling a country and sending your own people to live there
reforms, changes that improve a system

Florence Nightingale

Florence Nightingale (1820–1910) came from a wealthy English family. Against her parents' wishes, she became a nurse.

In 1853, she became superintendent of a hospital for women in London. In 1854, Britain, France, and Turkey fought against Russia in the Crimean War. Nightingale volunteered to go to Turkey to help. She took thirty-eight nurses with her. They helped many wounded soldiers recover. Nightingale often visited the soldiers at night, carrying a lamp. Soldiers called her "the lady with the lamp."

When Nightingale returned to England, she started a school for nurses. The school still exists today.

Mohandas Gandhi

Mohandas Gandhi (1869–1948) was born in the coastal city of Porbandar, in the western part of India. At that time, India was a British colony. Gandhi went to England in 1888 and studied law. He returned to India and worked as a lawyer in Bombay (Mumbai).

---

wealthy, very rich

Comprehension Check

Underline the sentence that tells what Florence Nightingale did against her parents' wishes. Why might she have chosen to do this with her life?

_____

_____

_____

Reading Strategy: Identify Problems and Solutions

Circle the sentence that tells what Florence Nightingale did when the Crimean War broke out. What problem was she helping to solve?

_____

_____

_____

Text Structure

Social Studies articles often give the year when a person was born and the year he or she died. Circle the year when Gandhi died. How old was he when he died?

_____

_____

Reading Strategy: Identify Problems and Solutions

Underline the sentence in the first paragraph that explains apartheid. What was Gandhi's response to this problem?

Mark the Text

_____

_____

_____

Comprehension Check

Circle two violent things that the text says happened to Gandhi. Why do you think Gandhi thought nonviolent protest was best?

Mark the Text

_____

_____

_____

Text Structure

Important words are often highlighted in social studies articles. Their definitions are provided at the bottom of the page. Circle the highlighted word in the third paragraph. Write a new sentence using the word.

Mark the Text

_____

_____

_____

In 1893, Gandhi traveled to South Africa. The government of South Africa had a system of racial separation, called apartheid. A group of white South Africans attacked Gandhi and beat him. After this experience, he encouraged people to practice passive resistance against the South African authorities and apartheid.

After he returned to India in 1915, Gandhi became a leader in India's struggle for independence. He became the international symbol of nonviolent protest. He believed in religious tolerance. In 1947, Britain finally ended its 190-year rule in India. Then, in 1948, Gandhi was assassinated by someone who didn't agree with his beliefs.

Gandhi inspired nonviolent movements elsewhere. In the United States, Dr. Martin Luther King Jr. used passive resistance when he became leader of the civil rights movement in the 1950s and 1960s.

---

apartheid, a system in which different races in a country are separated
inspired, caused; influenced people to express interest in

Franklin Delano Roosevelt

Franklin Delano Roosevelt (1882–1945) was elected as the thirty-second president of the United States in 1932. During the 1930s, the country was experiencing deep economic troubles. This period in American history is called the Great Depression. Banks shut down, workers lost their jobs, and farms failed. Roosevelt declared that Americans had "nothing to fear but fear itself." He put into place a series of new government programs that brought hope to the American people. Many people returned to work.

Roosevelt soon faced another challenge. The Second World War in Europe and the Pacific began in 1939. Great Britain, France, Russia, and other countries (the Allies) fought against Germany and Japan. In 1941, the Japanese bombed Pearl Harbor in Hawaii. Roosevelt declared war on Japan, and the United States entered the war. The United States and the Allies fought many brave battles and eventually won the war in 1945.

Roosevelt faced personal challenges as well. He came down with polio at the age of thirty-nine, and lost the use of his legs. However, Roosevelt did not allow his physical condition to prevent him from contributing to society. Roosevelt is now considered by many historians to be one of the greatest U.S. presidents.

---

economic, relating to business, industry, and managing money
polio, an infectious disease of the nerves in the spine that can cause paralysis

Reading Strategy: Identify Problems and Solutions

The Great Depression was a huge problem for the United States. Underline the sentence that tells what happened during the Great Depression. What was President Roosevelt's solution to this problem?

_____

_____

_____

Comprehension Check

Circle Roosevelt's words that are quoted on this page. What do you think Roosevelt meant by these words?

_____

_____

_____

Text Structure

The last sentence of a section often sums up the main idea of that section. Underline the last sentence on this page. In your own words, why is Roosevelt considered one of the greatest U.S. presidents?

_____

_____

_____

Reading Strategy: Identify Problems and Solutions

Underline what the text says happened to Helen Keller because of her illness when she was young. How did Helen Keller and Anne Sullivan solve the problems caused by this early illness?

_____

_____

_____

Comprehension Check

Underline what the text says about how Helen Keller helped others. In what way did she inspire others?

_____

_____

_____

Text Structure

Social studies articles often have highlighted words. Their definitions are provided at the bottom of the page. Circle the highlighted word in the last paragraph. Look at its definition. Reread the sentence in which it appears. Rewrite the sentence without using the highlighted word.

_____

_____

_____

Helen Keller

Helen Keller (1880–1968) was nineteen months old when she became sick with a fever. The sickness left her without sight or hearing. Because she was so young when this happened, it was hard for her to learn to communicate. Because she could not see, she was unable to use sign language—the language of hearing-impaired people. She also couldn't "read lips," as many hearing-impaired people do. Although these challenges made young Helen very frustrated, she was also extremely intelligent. With the help of a skilled teacher, named Anne Sullivan, she learned that everything had a name and that these names were words. Because of the help of others and her own determination, she was eventually able to learn different ways to communicate. For instance, she learned to "hear" and understand speech by touching a speaker's lips and throat.

Keller gave lectures (with her teacher's help) and wrote a number of books. Her public talks and her writings inspired countless people with hearing, sight, and other physical problems. She inspired others to not give up in the face of adversity. Keller also toured the world. She raised funds for programs to help people with impaired hearing and sight. To this day, Helen Keller remains a figure of inspiration.

---

impaired, damaged, or less strong, or less good
frustrated, upset because you can't do something
adversity, difficulties or problems

Doctors Without Borders

Doctors Without Borders is an international organization whose members believe that every person in every country has the right to medical care. It helps victims of war, disease, and natural disasters. A small group of French doctors started Doctors Without Borders (Médecins Sans Frontières) in 1971. Each year, thousands of volunteer doctors, nurses, and administrators from countries all over the world provide medical aid to people in more than seventy countries. They provide health care, perform surgery, organize nutrition and sanitation programs, train local medical staff, and provide mental health care.

Doctors Without Borders works with the United Nations, governments, and the media to tell the world about their patients' suffering and concerns. For example, Doctors Without Borders volunteers told the media about the atrocities they saw in Chechnya, Angola, and Kosovo.

Doctors Without Borders won the Nobel Peace Prize in 1999. Accepting the award, one of the organization's founders, Bernard Kouchner, said, "I'm deeply moved, and I'm thinking of all the people who died without aid, of all those who died waiting for someone to knock on their door."

---

borders, official lines that separate two countries
administrators, people who manage businesses or
    organizations
nutrition, food for good health and growth
sanitation, hygiene; cleanliness
atrocities, extremely violent actions

Text Structure

Social studies articles often include headings that tell you what a section is about. **Mark the Text**
Circle the heading on this page. What question do you think this section will answer?

_____

_____

_____

Reading Strategy: Identify Problems and Solutions

Doctors Without Borders solves a problem for people all over the world. **Mark the Text**
Underline three sentences that describe ways in which Doctors Without Borders solves this problem. In your own words, describe what Doctors Without Borders does.

_____

_____

_____

Choose one and complete:

1. Use library sources or the Internet to learn more about one of the people in this article. Prepare a one-page report and present it to your class.

2. Brainstorm with a group about ways students like you can help other people. Make a list of the group's ideas.

3. Write a short song about one of the people described in the article.

Retell It!

Imagine you are a friend of one of the people in this article. Write a paragraph describing your friend's career.

_____

_____

_____

_____

_____

_____

_____

_____

Reader's Response

Sometimes people help others even though it puts them in danger. Do you think you would be able to do that? Why or why not?

_____

_____

_____

_____

_____

Think About the Skill

How did identifying problems and solutions help you better understand the article?

_____

_____

_____

_____

EDIT FOR MEANING

Read

You have read "Extraordinary People: Serving Others." Now read one paragraph from it again.

Doctors Without Borders

Doctors Without Borders is an international organization whose members believe that every person in every country has the right to medical care. It helps victims of war, disease, and natural disasters. A small group of French doctors started Doctors Without Borders (Médecins Sans Frontières) in 1971. Each year, thousands of volunteer doctors, nurses, and administrators from countries all over the world provide medical aid to people in more than seventy countries. They provide health care, perform surgery, organize nutrition and sanitation programs, train local medical staff, and provide mental health care.

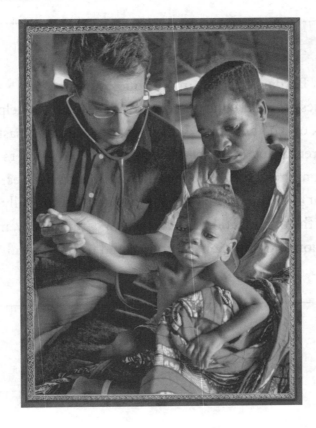

Fix the Error

Each paragraph below contains the same information as the paragraph you just read. However, each paragraph contains one error. First, find the error. Then fix it by editing the sentence so that the information is correct.

1. Find and fix the error.

Doctors Without Borders

Doctors Without Borders is a worldwide organization. Its members believe that everyone should have medical care. Victims of war, disease, and natural disasters help them. The organization was started in France in 1971. People from more than seventy countries are treated each year by thousands of doctors, nurses, and administrators from countries all over the world. The organization provides medical care, performs surgery, and offers mental health care.

2. Find and fix the error.

Doctors Without Borders

Doctors Without Borders operates in only one country. The organization believes that everyone deserves to see a doctor. It helps people who are sick or who are injured due to war or natural disasters. A small group of French doctors started Doctors Without Borders (Médecins Sans Frontières) in 1971. Thousands of doctors, nurses, and administrators treat people in more than seventy nations annually. Services offered by the organization include health care, surgery, mental health care, sanitation and nutrition programs, and training local doctors and nurses.

Name _____ Date _____

Crossword Puzzle

To complete this crossword puzzle, you'll need to remember or search for details in the reading. Use the words in the word box. Not all of the words in the word box are in the puzzle. Fill in the crossword with answers to the clues below. The first answer has been done for you.

Word box:
JAPANESE
POLIO
SULLIVAN
FRENCH
ALLIES
~~KOUCHNER~~
NOBEL
MALARIA
TURKEY
KING
INDIA
ZAPOTEC

Across

3. The disease Franklin Delano Roosevelt developed
6. Helen Keller's teacher
9. People who tried to colonize Mexico
10. Great Britain, France, Russia, and the United States were called this when they fought against Germany and Japan

Down

1. A founder of Doctors Without Borders
2. Peace prize won by Doctors Without Borders
4. Country where Florence Nightingale treated wounded soldiers
5. A man influenced by Gandhi to use passive resistance
7. Home country of Mohandas Gandhi
8. The kind of Indian Benito Juárez was

1. Silently read the text below. Make sure you understand the point that each sentence is making.

2. Underline the word or words in each sentence that are most important. When you read, you should say these underlined words with expression.

3. Look again at the punctuation in the paragraphs. Remember that when a sentence ends in a period, you should read the words as a statement and take a breath before beginning a new sentence. When you see a comma, you should pause briefly. When you see an exclamation mark, you should sound excited. When you see a question mark, you should read as though you are asking a question.

4. Now read the paragraphs below out loud. Pay attention to the important words and punctuation as you read.

5. Write down any words that slowed you down. Practice saying these words out loud.

6. Read the text below out loud two more times. You may want to ask a friend or family member to listen to you and tell you their reactions to your reading.

Helen Keller

Helen Keller (1880–1968) was nineteen months old when she became sick with a fever. The sickness left her without sight or hearing. Because she was so young when this happened, it was hard for her to learn to communicate. Because she could not see, she was unable to use sign language—the language of hearing-impaired people. She also couldn't "read lips," as many hearing-impaired people do. Although these challenges made young Helen very frustrated, she was also extremely intelligent. With the help of a skilled teacher, named Anne Sullivan, she learned that everything had a name and that these names were words. Because of the help of others and her own determination, she was eventually able to learn different ways to communicate. For instance, she learned to "hear" and understand speech by touching a speaker's lips and throat.

Name _____ Date _____

UNIT 3

How does helping others help us all?

READING 4: "Friendship and Cooperation in the Animal Kingdom"

SUMMARY *Use with textbook pages 180–183.*

This passage tells about two ways in which animals help each other: symbiosis and friendship. Symbiosis is a type of relationship between animals in which the animals depend on each other for survival. For example, crocodiles let small birds called plovers clean their teeth. The crocodiles' teeth get cleaned and the plovers get an easy meal. It is a symbiotic relationship because the animals benefit from each other. Occasionally, animals simply enjoy being with each other and become friends. This happened with a baby hippo named Owen and an old tortoise named Mzee. Owen lost his mother. At an animal shelter, Owen and Mzee became very good friends and refused to be separated.

Visual Summary

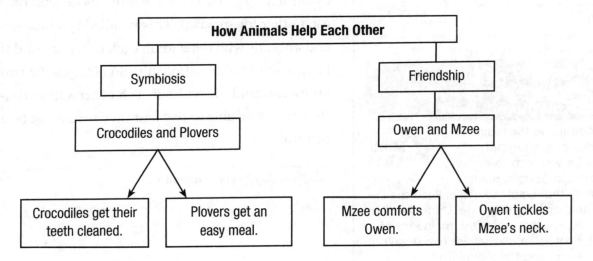

Use What You Know

List three ways different animals can help each other.

1. _____

2. _____

3. _____

Text Structure

A science article always begins with a title. Circle the title on this page. What do you think the article will be about?

Mark the Text

_____

_____

_____

Reading Strategy: Identify Main Idea and Supporting Details

Identifying the main idea of a paragraph helps you recognize the most important points an author wants to make. Read the last paragraph on the page. Underline the sentence that states the main idea of the paragraph. What are two details that support the main idea?

Mark the Text

1. _____

2. _____

Friendship and Cooperation in the Animal Kingdom

You know that people help other people, but do animals help other animals? It's a "dog-eat-dog" world out there, isn't it? Not always! It's true that animals often fight. However, at other times they help each other out.

Life in the wild can be very difficult for animals. It is not easy for them to find food and water and stay safe. Animals struggle every day to survive.

That's why animals of the same species, or group, such as lions or blue jays, sometimes cooperate. By helping one another, they help their group survive.

Some animals become partners with other kinds of animals. The two types of animals depend on each other for survival. This is called symbiosis, and animals who depend on each other are said to be in a symbiotic relationship. Sometimes the two animals would die without each other. Other times, they might be able to live, but they would not be as healthy.

"**dog-eat-dog**," very competitive

One example of symbiosis is the relationship between the plover and the crocodile. The plover is a small wading bird. It helps pick clean the Nile crocodile's body and even its teeth. The crocodile will open its jaws and let the bird enter its mouth safely. Amazingly, the crocodile will not snap its jaws shut. Instead, it patiently allows the plover to eat the small, harmful animals on the crocodile's teeth. The crocodile gets its teeth cleaned, and the plover gets an easy meal!

Symbiosis is a working relationship. Many animal species have worked out this arrangement with other animal species. Sometimes, however, animals simply become friends with other animals. There may not be an obvious reason. Perhaps they just like the companionship.

Animals can find friends in the strangest places. For an example, take Owen, a baby hippopotamus. It is hard to believe, but Owen actually became best friends with a 318-kilogram (700-lb.) tortoise named Mzee (mm-ZAY).

Text Structure

Science articles often provide an example to explain a key word. Circle the key word in the first sentence and underline the example the writer gives to explain this term. How would you explain the relationship between the plover and the crocodile?

_____

_____

_____

Reading Strategy: Identify Main Idea and Supporting Details

Identifying supporting details helps you remember main ideas by forming a picture in your mind about what you are reading. Circle the details in the first paragraph. What main idea does the author want you to remember?

_____

_____

_____

Comprehension Check

Circle the paragraph that discusses the difference between symbiosis and friendship. How is friendship between animals different from symbiotic relationships between animal species?

_____

_____

_____

Owen, the hippo, lived in the country of Kenya on the east coast of Africa. He was just one year old, and he already weighed 272 kilograms (600 lb.). He lived happily with his mother in a group of about twenty hippos. They grazed on the grass along the Sabaki River near the small village of Malindi.

On December 26, 2004, a disaster struck. There was a huge earthquake under the ocean floor near Indonesia. This caused a gigantic tsunami. The tsunami wiped out towns and villages throughout Asia. Around 230,000 people died. By the time the tsunami reached the east coast of Africa, the waves had lost a great deal of power. However, they still caused flooding and widespread damage. Owen had been swimming in the river with his mother when the tsunami hit. The enormous waves separated Owen from his mother and swept him out to sea.

The next day, the people of Malindi saw the struggling baby hippo, without its mother, stranded on a coral reef. It was Owen. He was tired and frightened. Owen could not reach the shore on his own. It took hours for the villagers to rescue Owen from the coral reef.

But what should they do with a 272-kilogram (600-lb.) baby hippo? The people could not return him to the wild. Owen had not yet learned to take care of himself. Another hippo group would not accept him. Other hippos would think Owen was an intruder and probably attack him.

Luckily for Owen, there was an animal shelter nearby named Haller Park. The workers prepared a perfect home for Owen. It had a pond, a mud hole, tall trees, and lots of grass. This seemed perfect for a hippo, but Owen's new home was not empty. Some monkeys and a 318-kilogram tortoise named Mzee (mm-ZAY) already lived in Haller Park.

It took hours for the people of Malindi to load Owen into a pickup truck. Owen was very angry, and he was also very frightened. He had lost his mother and his friends. He did not know where he was or where he was going.

---

coral reef, line of hard material formed by the skeletons of small ocean creatures that live in warm water

Comprehension Check

Underline the sentence in the first paragraph that tells what Owen's problem was. Why do you think Owen was not able to live on his own without his mother?

_____

_____

_____

Text Structure

Science articles often include highlighted words that are defined at the bottom of the page. Circle the highlighted term on this page. Read its definition. How do you think the hippo could have ended up on the coral reef?

_____

_____

_____

Reading Strategy: Identify Main Idea and Supporting Details

Identifying main ideas and details can help you understand what is most important to remember from what you read. Read the third paragraph and underline its main idea. List three details about Haller Park.

1. _____

2. _____

3. _____

When Owen arrived at Haller Park, he quickly left the pickup truck and ran right to Mzee. The workers looked in amazement when Owen quickly hid behind the giant tortoise. This is exactly the way a baby hippo would hide behind its mother if it felt the need for protection.

Mzee was shocked and surprised. He had originally come from Aldabra Island. This is part of the country of Seychelles in the Indian Ocean. Sailors had probably taken Mzee from his home to be used for food. He must have escaped from the ship, maybe during a shipwreck, and come ashore somewhere on the eastern coast of Africa. That was a long time before, because Mzee was about 130 years old. (Some giant tortoises live to be 200 years old!)

Mzee must have seen a lot in his long life. Like most giant tortoises, he was not very friendly. He preferred to be left alone. So, at first, Mzee tried to crawl away from Owen. However, as you know, tortoises cannot move very quickly. Owen just watched where Mzee went and then followed him around. For some reason, Mzee began to like his new companion.

Over the next few days, the two giant animals became good friends. Then they became great friends. In fact, Owen and Mzee soon refused to be separated. They would spend all their time together, eating, swimming, sleeping, and playing. Mzee would stretch out his neck and Owen would tickle it. At night, the two huge animals would cuddle up next to each other. Mzee and Owen even developed their own way of "talking" with each other.

It is a bit of a mystery why Owen and Mzee became such good friends. After all, Owen is a mammal and Mzee is a reptile. Perhaps Mzee's coloring and round shape reminded Owen of his mother. Maybe Owen looked like another tortoise to Mzee. For whatever reason, they surprised scientists with the strength of their friendship.

Mzee's name means "wise man" in Swahili (one of the main languages of Kenya). It turned out that Mzee's name was well chosen. When Owen the hippo needed a friend, Mzee was there for him. Owen suffered a tremendous loss, but he never gave up. He kept trying and now has a happy life.

---

tickle, touch a person or animal lightly, often in order to make him or her laugh

Choose one and complete:

1. Use an atlas at the library or on the Internet to find some of the places mentioned in the article. Mark the places you find in your research on a map of the world.

2. Draw a picture of Owen and Mzee. At the bottom, list some of the things they like to do together. Give your picture a title.

3. Write a song or poem about Owen and Mzee's friendship.

Reading Strategy: Identify Main Idea and Supporting Details

Underline the sentences that tell the main idea of the first paragraph. What details are given to show that Owen and Mzee became great friends?

Mark the Text

1. _____

2. _____

3. _____

4. _____

Text Structure

Circle the highlighted word on this page and read its definition at the bottom of the page. Write your own sentence using the word.

Mark the Text

_____

_____

_____

Comprehension Check

Circle the words in the second paragraph that tell what kind of animal Owen is and what kind of animal Mzee is. Why do you think it is unusual for a mammal and a reptile to be friends?

Mark the Text

_____

_____

_____

_____

Retell It!

Retell the story of how Owen and Mzee became friends in your own words.

_____

_____

_____

_____

_____

_____

_____

Reader's Response

The people of Malindi worked for hours to rescue Owen from the coral reef where he was stranded. What do their efforts tell us about the people of Malindi?

_____

_____

_____

_____

Think About the Skill

How did identifying the main idea and supporting details of some paragraphs help you to better understand the article?

_____

_____

_____

_____

EDIT FOR MEANING

Read

You have read "Friendship and Cooperation in the Animal Kingdom." Now read one paragraph from it again.

Friendship and Cooperation in the Animal Kingdom

One example of symbiosis is the relationship between the plover and the crocodile. The plover is a small wading bird. It helps pick clean the Nile crocodile's body and even its teeth. The crocodile will open its jaws and let the bird enter its mouth safely. Amazingly, the crocodile will not snap its jaws shut. Instead, it patiently allows the plover to eat the small, harmful animals on the crocodile's teeth. The crocodile gets its teeth cleaned, and the plover gets an easy meal!

Fix the Error

Each paragraph below contains the same information as the paragraph you just read. However, each paragraph contains one error. First, find the error. Then fix it by editing the sentence so that the information is correct.

1. Find and fix the error.

Friendship and Cooperation in the Animal Kingdom

The relationship between the plover and the crocodile is an example of symbiosis. A small wading bird, the plover eats from the Nile crocodile's teeth and body. The crocodile opens its mouth and lets the bird in safely. Amazingly, the crocodile never closes its mouth on the bird. Instead, the crocodile calmly allows the plover to eat from its teeth. No one knows what benefit there might be to the crocodile, but the plover gets an easy meal.

---

2. Find and fix the error.

Friendship and Cooperation in the Animal Kingdom

The crocodile and the plover have a symbiotic relationship. The plover, which is a small bird, helps pick clean the Nile crocodile's teeth. The crocodile opens its jaws and lets the bird enter its mouth. Amazingly, the plover does this even though sometimes the crocodile shuts its jaws with a snap and eats the bird. The plover quickly eats whatever it finds on the crocodile's teeth. The crocodile provides the plover with a meal and gets its teeth cleaned in exchange!

FOCUS ON DETAILS

Word Search Puzzle

To complete this word search puzzle, you'll need to remember or search for details in the reading. Look at the clues and circle the answers in the puzzle below. Check off each clue after you've found the answer. Write each word next to its clue.

1. ☑ Enormous wave that wiped out towns and villages _____
2. ☐ Village where people rescued Owen _____
3. ☐ The bird that cleans crocodiles' teeth _____
4. ☐ Country where Owen lived with his mother _____
5. ☐ The kind of reptile Mzee is _____
6. ☐ Event that caused the tsunami _____
7. ☐ The other animals living at Haller Park _____
8. ☐ Language Mzee's name is from _____
9. ☐ Animal shelter where Owen and Mzee live _____
10. ☐ Name of the island Mzee was from _____

```
P  A  V  M  S  K  X  F  E  S  B  L  F  T  C
T  C  A  O  S  T  D  T  Z  W  K  E  N  Y  A
O  S  H  E  A  E  U  O  G  A  N  J  E  Y  U
Z  T  U  Y  L  U  G  R  D  H  X  U  M  F  V
L  A  W  N  D  Z  K  T  P  I  L  K  A  O  B
A  I  V  Y  A  A  W  O  V  L  R  C  L  P  H
T  W  Q  X  B  M  Q  I  T  I  E  N  I  S  A
P  M  H  E  R  D  I  S  T  M  Z  F  N  Y  L
L  L  A  K  A  G  Z  E  H  S  E  O  D  W  L
B  B  O  I  F  M  D  H  R  Q  O  G  I  P  E
N  B  R  V  I  X  C  E  B  I  T  R  H  R  R
P  J  R  N  E  G  M  O  N  K  E  Y  S  L  P
Y  R  C  L  S  R  H  N  C  U  T  K  Q  I  A
J  E  A  R  T  H  Q  U  A  K  E  I  S  S  R
W  K  Q  J  V  M  O  Y  J  D  N  L  X  Z  K
```

READ FOR FLUENCY

1. Silently read the text below. Make sure you understand the point that each sentence is making.

2. Underline the word or words in each sentence that are most important. When you read, you should say these underlined words with expression.

3. Look again at the punctuation in the paragraphs. Remember that when a sentence ends in a period, you should read the words as a statement and take a breath before beginning a new sentence. When you see a comma, you should pause briefly. When you see an exclamation mark, you should sound excited. When you see a question mark, you should read as though you are asking a question.

4. Now read the paragraphs below out loud. Pay attention to the important words and punctuation as you read.

5. Write down any words that slowed you down. Practice saying these words out loud.

6. Read the text below out loud two more times. You may want to ask a friend or family member to listen to you and tell you their reactions to your reading.

Friendship and Cooperation in the Animal Kingdom

You know that people help other people, but do animals help other animals? It's a "dog-eat-dog" world out there, isn't it? Not always! It's true that animals often fight. However, at other times they help each other out.

Life in the wild can be very difficult for animals. It is not easy for them to find food and water and stay safe. Animals struggle every day to survive.

That's why animals of the same species, or group, such as lions or blue jays, sometimes cooperate. By helping one another, they help their group survive.

Name _____ Date _____

What do we learn through winning and losing?

READING 1: "Soccer: The World Sport"

SUMMARY   *Use with textbook pages 204–209.*

Soccer is the world's most popular game. Its rules are simple and you need very little equipment to play. The article tells about the history of soccer and how the modern game of soccer developed. Today, soccer is the fastest-growing team sport in the U.S. Interest in soccer increased greatly after the U.S. national team won the 1999 Women's World Cup in California. There is another reason for soccer's growing popularity. Many soccer-playing immigrants have come to the United States over the past ten to fifteen years. The article tells about one team, the Fugees. The players are young refugees living in Georgia. They came from very different countries, but they all share a love for soccer.

Visual Summary

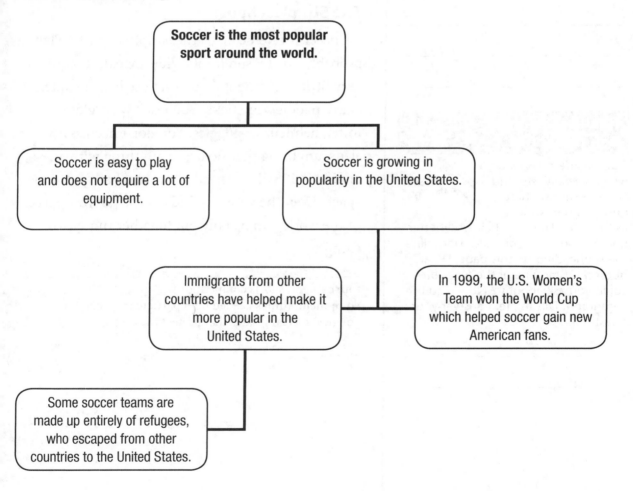

Use What You Know

List three sports you like to play or watch.

1. _____

2. _____

3. _____

Text Structure

The title of this social studies article includes a subtitle. A subtitle usually appears after a colon. It provides extra information about the topic. Circle the subtitle on this page. What does it tell you about the sport of soccer?

_____

_____

_____

Reading Strategy: Ask Questions

Good readers ask *who, what, when, where,* and *why* questions. These questions are known as the 5Ws. They can help you better understand what you read. Underline the subheading on this page. What question using one of the 5W words could you ask about it? Now read the paragraph. Did the text answer your question?

_____

_____

"Soccer: The World Sport"

Americans call the game *soccer*. The British, and almost everyone else in the world, call it *football*. Under either name, soccer has become the most popular sport in the world. It is played almost everywhere. More than 200 countries have national professional teams. Every four years, more people watch the final game of the World Cup tournament on TV than any other sporting event. In 2006, the TV audience was 1.3 billion viewers. Compare that to the Superbowl—the most-watched sports program in the United States. American football, however, is not a major sport in any other country—only 95 million people watched it.

The Simplest Sport

Soccer is often called "the simplest sport." That's probably one reason for its wide appeal. It requires very little equipment. You don't use bats, racquets, clubs, paddles, or sticks. You don't wear gloves, mitts, helmets, or goggles. You don't need skis, sleds, anything that floats, or anything with an engine in it. All you need is a round ball and some space. Even the youngest kids in the poorest parts of the world can usually put together those two things.

---

tournament, sports competition
equipment, things needed for a particular activity
goggles, special glasses that protect the eyes

The rules of the game are also simple. Two teams of eleven players each try to get the ball into the other team's goal. You can kick the ball or use your head to move it. No one except the goalkeeper (or "goalie") is allowed to touch the ball with hands or arms. This is what makes soccer unique among sports. Think about it. Even in everyday life, what actions do you perform *without* using your hands? The answer is: none or almost none. It's certainly true in sports. You are always using your hands in sports. You *hit, shoot, pass,* and *carry.* You *serve, dunk, rebound,* and *throw.* Even in the simple childhood game of "tag," you have to *tag* the other players to get them out!

There is an old saying: "Necessity is the mother of invention." This means that if people need something, they will find a way to invent it. The rules of soccer took away the use of the players' hands. This forced soccer players to "invent" new ways to use their feet. Soccer players don't just *pass* the ball with their feet. They *protect* it, *block* it, and *steal* it from their opponents. Their footwork is so fast and so skillful that sometimes it's hard to follow without replaying the action in slow motion. In addition, players often dazzle audiences with leaping kicks that are as awesome as the flying dunks of professional basketball players.

---

goal, area in which you try to put the ball to win a point
goalkeeper, player on a team who tries to stop the ball before
  it goes into the goal
dunk, jump up and slam the ball from above into the basket
  in a game of basketball
rebound, catch a basketball after a player has tried but failed
  to get a point
necessity, being in need
dazzle, amaze with an inspiring display

Reading Strategy: Ask Questions

Circle the text in the first paragraph that tells the rules of soccer. **Mark the Text** What are two questions you might ask to find out more about the game of soccer?

1. _____

2. _____

Comprehension Check

Underline the text that provides another name for the goalkeeper. **Mark the Text** What can he or she do that other players cannot?

_____

_____

_____

Text Structure

A social studies article often has highlighted vocabulary words. **Mark the Text** Their definitions are at the bottom of the page. Circle the highlighted vocabulary word at the bottom of the second paragraph. Look at its definition. Rewrite the sentence in which it appears without using the vocabulary word.

_____

_____

_____

A Little History

No one knows exactly where or when soccer began. Written records from 2,000 years ago in China describe games in which a ball was kicked into a goal. Other records have been found in Japan, Greece, and Italy.

The modern game of soccer was developed from the eighth to the nineteenth century in England. In 1863, a formal set of rules was adopted. Other countries accepted these rules, and soon international matches were held. At this time, Great Britain ruled colonies all over the world, and British traders, soldiers, and sailors introduced the game to many parts of Asia, Africa, and the Americas.

The *Fédération Internationale de Football Association* (FIFA) was formed in 1904. It is still the governing body of the sport. By 1930, there were professional football leagues in many countries. The first World Cup tournament was held in Uruguay in 1930. It has been held every four years since then.

---

traders, people who buy and sell goods

A Big Boom

Today, about 18 million people play soccer in the United States. It is the fastest growing team sport in the country. Major League Soccer (MLS) was started in 1996, after other professional soccer leagues had failed. The goal of MLS is to make soccer into a mainstream sport like football, baseball, and basketball.

One big boost was the 1999 Women's World Cup played at the Rose Bowl in Palo Alto, California. The U.S. Women's National Team beat China in front of a crowd of 90,185, the largest number of people at a women's sports event ever. The teams were scoreless in regulation time, scoreless in overtime, and the U.S. finally won 5-4 in penalty kicks. Brandi Chastain scored the winning point, and her picture was on the cover of many sports magazines and newspapers. People who had never followed soccer watched this game on television, and the sport began to attract many new fans.

Something Bigger Than Winning

Most athletes play sports because they want to win. Why else would the players put in hours of practice and travel? Why would they sacrifice their social life and money and sleep to help their team get better and better?

---

mainstream, popular; accepted
regulation time, the normal period of time in which a soccer game is played; 90 minutes
overtime, the period of time added to the end of a sports game to give one of the two teams a chance to win
penalty kicks, chances to kick the ball into the goal that are given because the other team has not obeyed a rule

Reading Strategy: Ask Questions

Read the first two paragraphs on this page. Then write a 5W question you could ask to learn more about soccer in the United States today. (Make sure that your question starts with one of these words: who, what, when, where, or why.)

_____

_____

Comprehension Check

Circle the year when the MLS started. Why do you think this league was created?

_____

_____

_____

Text Structure

A social studies article often presents important facts or figures. Circle the sentence that tells how many people attended the Women's World Cup in 1999. Why was this match so important?

_____

_____

_____

But, if winning is the only goal, most teams will feel like losers, because there can be only one winner at the end of each season.

Is there something about soccer—as it's played in the United States at this time in history—that goes beyond winning and losing? The answer doesn't come from the game, but from the people who play it. The wave of immigrants to the United States in the last ten to fifteen years has been a big part of the soccer boom. These newcomers have arrived from Central and South America, Africa, and parts of Asia. Many have come from countries torn apart by war, poverty, and natural disasters. Soccer is important to people already in the United States, but it has an even deeper meaning to many recent refugees. For them, soccer can sometimes be a lifeline.

One example of this is a team in Clarkston, Georgia, a small town outside of Atlanta. In 2004, a soccer team was organized. It is made up entirely of refugees. In fact, the team calls itself the Fugees (as in re**fugees**). The players are all in this country legally, brought by a resettlement agency because of housing and low-paying jobs nearby.

---

refugees, people who have left their country, especially because of a war
lifeline, something that someone depends on completely
resettlement agency, organization that helps refugees adjust to life in the United States

The reporter Warren St. John wrote about the Fugees in the *New York Times*. The boys, all between eight and thirteen, have come from Sudan, Somalia, Bosnia, Iraq, and Afghanistan. Some lived for years in refugee camps. Some have been separated from their families. Some watched their loved ones taken away to prison. One boy saw his father murdered in their home. They have been through a lot in their young lives.

One day a young coach named Luma Mufleh put up a sign announcing tryouts for a soccer team. The team was to be for refugees only, and she was going to be the coach. Those who made the team had to sign a contract accepting certain responsibilities on and off the field. They were going to have to work really hard, but they would have the chance to do something they loved. Before they played their first game, the boys had already "won" several important things: respect, a group they could belong to, and the chance to do really well at something.

---

tryouts, times when people who want to be on a sports team are tested so that the best can be chosen

---

Reading Strategy: Ask Questions

Underline the name of the person who wrote about the Fugees. Imagine you are a newspaper reporter about to interview the Fugees. Write down two *when*, *where*, or *why* questions you might ask members of the team.

Mark the Text

1. _____

2. _____

Text Structure

Social studies articles often focus on history, but can also include geography. Geography is the study of places around the world. Underline all the names of the countries that players on the Fugees team came from. What was one of the hardships they faced?

Mark the Text

_____

_____

_____

Comprehension Check

Circle the sentence that tells what the team members had to sign. What were they accepting by signing the contract?

Mark the Text

_____

_____

_____

The season wasn't perfect. The Fugees did not win every game. The tragedies they had experienced in the past did not suddenly disappear. But other teams admired the way the Fugees played. Parents from the wealthier teams helped the Fugees buy balls, uniforms, and cleated shoes. The boys on the team learned to work together. They had come from different countries, but they all shared a love of soccer. They got to know one another through the sport, and the sport is helping them all to bridge the gap from their old world to their new one.

---

tragedies, events that cause a lot of sadness
wealthier, richer, having more money
cleated, shoes that have short pieces of rubber, plastic, or metal attached to the bottom of them, in order to prevent someone from slipping
bridge the gap, reduce or get rid of the difference between two things

Name _____ Date _____

Comprehension Check

Underline the sentences that tell what soccer is doing throughout cities and towns. What is one reason why soccer can have a powerful effect on people's lives?

Mark the Text

_____

_____

_____

Reading Strategy: Ask Questions

Circle the subheading that appears on this page. Create a question with one of the 5Ws (who, what, when, where, or why) that you could ask about this section.

Mark the Text

_____

_____

Text Structure

Draw a box around the last highlighted vocabulary word on this page. Look at the definition. Then write a new sentence using the vocabulary word.

Mark the Text

_____

_____

_____

Throughout U.S. cities and towns soccer is working its magic. It may be "the simplest game," but soccer can have a powerful effect on people's lives. No other sport crosses over so many cultural, racial, and ethnic boundaries as soccer.

A Different Ending Every Time

It's true that all sports are different, but they all have one thing in common: Every game is like a story written right there on the spot. It's never the same story, and no one knows the ending ahead of time.

You might lose today, but there will be another game tomorrow. Soccer has attracted millions of fans and created millions of players. Most will never make it to the professional leagues, but they'll probably make some friends, have fun, and experience the satisfaction of working hard to meet a goal. That's not bad for a simple game!

_____

on the spot, immediately, without careful planning
satisfaction, feeling of happiness or pleasure because of an achievement

Choose one and complete:

1. Create a poster that explains the rules of soccer. Cut out photographs from magazines or draw pictures to include on your poster.

2. On an outline map of the world, highlight some of the countries refugees left to come to the United States. Then do research in the library or on the Internet to learn about one of them. Write two or three paragraphs to tell about the hardships refugees faced there.

3. Imagine you are a newspaper reporter attending the Women's World Cup in 1999. Write a short article about the game. You might need to do extra research about the tournament at the library or on the Internet.

Retell It!

Soccer is often called "the simplest sport." Explain why it is called that.

_____

_____

_____

_____

_____

_____

_____

Reader's Response

Do you think soccer will become more popular than other sports in the United States? Explain why or why not.

_____

_____

_____

_____

_____

Think About the Skill

How did asking *who, what, when, where,* and *why* questions help you to better understand the article?

_____

_____

_____

_____

EDIT FOR MEANING

Read

You have read "Soccer: The World Sport." Now read one paragraph from it again.

"Soccer: The World Sport"

Americans call the game *soccer*. The British, and almost everyone else in the world, call it *football*. Under either name, soccer has become the most popular sport in the world. It is played almost everywhere. More than 200 countries have national professional teams. Every four years, more people watch the final game of the World Cup tournament on TV than any other sporting event. In 2006, the TV audience was 1.3 billion viewers. Compare that to the Superbowl—the most-watched sports program in the United States. American football, however, is not a major sport in any other country—only 95 million people watched it.

Fix the Error

Each paragraph below contains the same information as the paragraph you just read. However, each paragraph contains one error. First, find the error. Then fix it by editing the sentence so the information is correct.

1. Find and fix the error.

"Soccer: The World Sport"

People in the United States call the game *soccer*. But in Great Britain and almost every other country, people call it *football*. Under either name, soccer is the least popular sport in the world. It is played almost everywhere. More than 200 countries have professional teams. Every four years, more people watch the final game of the World Cup on TV than any other sporting event. In 2006, the TV audience was 1.3 billion viewers. Compare that to the most-watched sports program in the United States—the Superbowl. Only 95 million people watched that game. But unlike soccer, American football is not a major sport in any other country.

---

2. Find and fix the error.

"Soccer: The World Sport"

People in the United States call it *soccer*. But in almost every other country around the globe, the sport is known as *football*. No matter what it is called, soccer is an extremely popular sport. For one thing, it is played almost everywhere. However, almost no countries have professional teams. Plus, every four years, more people watch the final game of the World Cup than any other sporting event. In 2006, 1.3 billion viewers saw it on television. Now think about the Superbowl that was played the same year. Only 95 million people watched that game. Why is the number of viewers so much smaller? Unlike soccer, American football is not a major sport around the world.

Name _____ Date _____

FOCUS on DETAILS

To complete this crossword puzzle, read the clues. Then choose words from the box.
Not all the words in the word box are answers to the puzzle. You can go back and
search for details in the reading to learn more about the words and clues below.

baseball	bats	eleven	England
fans	football	goalie	immigrants
Ireland	league	overtime	refugees
season	steal	television	throw

Across

1. The Fugees did not win every game during this.

5. This was started in the United States to make soccer more mainstream.

6. The modern game of soccer was developed here.

7. They helped soccer to become more popular in the United States.

9. The name for soccer in most of the world

Down

1. Players pass, protect, block, and do this with their feet.

2. The number of players on a soccer team

3. This is how more than one billion people watched the World Cup in 2006.

4. Another word for goalkeeper

8. Soccer is now attracting many of these in the United States.

1. Silently read the text below. Make sure you understand the point that each sentence is making.

2. Underline the word or words in each sentence that are most important. When you read, you should say these underlined words with expression.

3. Look again at the punctuation in the paragraphs. Remember that when a sentence ends in a period, you should read the words as a statement and take a breath before beginning a new sentence. When you see a comma, you should pause briefly. When you see an exclamation mark, you should sound excited. When you see a question mark, you should read as though you are asking a question.

4. Now read the paragraphs below out loud. Pay attention to the important words and punctuation as you read.

5. Write down any words that slowed you down. Practice saying these words out loud.

6. Read the text below out loud two more times. You may want to ask a friend or family member to listen to you and tell you their reactions to your reading.

The Simplest Sport

The rules of the game are also simple. Two teams of eleven players each try to get the ball into the other team's goal. You can kick the ball or use your head to move it. No one except the goalkeeper (or "goalie") is allowed to touch the ball with hands or arms. This is what makes soccer unique among sports. Think about it. Even in everyday life, what actions do you perform *without* using your hands? The answer is: none or almost none. It's certainly true in sports. You are always using your hands in sports. You *hit*, *shoot*, *pass*, and *carry*. You *serve*, *dunk*, *rebound*, and *throw*. Even in the simple childhood game of "tag," you have to *tag* the other players to get them out!

Name _____ Date _____

What do we learn through winning and losing?

READING 4: "Going, Going, Gone?"/
"Ivory-Billed Woodpeckers Make Noise"

SUMMARY *Use with textbook pages 244–247.*

The first article is about the extinction of birds. It tells about the ivory-billed
woodpecker. People thought the bird was extinct, but it may still exist. The article also
tells about the dodo, the passenger pigeon, and the Carolina parakeet. These birds are
now extinct because of human activity. Humans killed too many of them and destroyed
their environments. People also brought in animals from other areas. These nonnative
animals killed the birds. The second article tells about a recent sound recording made of
the ivory-billed woodpecker. After hearing the recording, scientists believe that the birds
still exist. The article describes a government plan to protect the birds' environment.

Visual Summary

Many birds have become extinct. They include the following species:			
The Ivory-Billed Woodpecker	*The Dodo*	*The Passenger Pigeon*	*The Carolina Parakeet*
• Loggers cut down trees where they lived. • Scientists rediscovered the ivory-billed woodpecker. • They made recordings of the bird's call. • Today, scientists work to protect these birds.	• Sailors hunted dodos, making them one of the first birds to become extinct.	• Settlers hunted the pigeons and killed them off.	• Farmers thought the birds were pests.

Going, Going, Gone?

When a species, or kind of animal, becomes extinct, it is lost forever. These online science articles both deal with birds that have become extinct. You will find out the effects that certain events and actions had on the dodo, the passenger pigeon, and the Carolina parakeet. You will also find out why some bird lovers now feel hopeful about a bird that was thought to be extinct. As you read, consider what can be done to prevent other living things from becoming extinct in the future.

More than eighty kinds of birds have died out, or become extinct, in the last 300 years. Some vanished because of natural causes. Humans killed off most of them. They hunted the birds too much and destroyed the birds' habitats. Read on for more details on the search for the ivory-billed woodpecker. (It might not be extinct as once thought.) Then check out the stories behind three extinct birds.

The Ivory-Billed Woodpecker

A team of bird experts is walking through mud and swamps in Louisiana's Pearl River forest. They hope to find the mysterious ivory-billed woodpecker. Experts believed this bird had been extinct for more than fifty years. A college student's sighting of unusual-looking birds sparked hopes that it might still be alive.

Loggers cut down trees in the Pearl River forest during the early 1800s. But some trees have grown back. There are now many old cypress, sweet gum, and oak trees that would serve as a good home for ivory-billed woodpeckers. The birds were known to eat the fat grubs that live under the bark of these trees. The researchers have already found trees with areas of bark that have been chipped off, as if by a large woodpecker. Only time will tell if it is an ivory-billed one.

_____

loggers, people whose job it is to cut down trees
grubs, insects when they are in the form of small, soft, white
    worms

Comprehension Check

Underline the sentence that tells where a team of experts was walking in Louisiana. What did the experts hope to find?

_____

_____

Reading Strategy: Recognize Cause and Effect

Underline the sentence that tells what loggers did to trees in the Pearl River forest. How did cutting the trees help make ivory-billed woodpeckers extinct?

_____

_____

Text Structure

A science article often has highlighted vocabulary words. Their definitions appear at the bottom of the page. Circle the second vocabulary word on this page. Look at its definition. Then write a new sentence using the vocabulary word.

_____

_____

_____

The Dodo

The dodo was the first bird to be wiped out by people during modern times. Dodos were large, flightless birds. They were first seen around 1600 on Mauritius, an island in the Indian Ocean. Less than eighty years later, the dodo was extinct. The dodo's heavy, clumsy body made it an easy target for sailors, who hunted it for food. As forests were destroyed, so was the dodo's food supply. And the cats, rats, pigs, and other predators unleashed by sailors preyed on the dodos. Together these factors led to the dodo's extinction.

_____

preyed on, hunted and ate

The Passenger Pigeon

These pigeons once lived in the eastern United States. They flew across this area in flocks so huge that they darkened the sky. In 1808 a single flock in Kentucky was estimated to contain over 2 billion birds. Today the passenger pigeon is extinct because of human activities. Settlers moving West during the nineteenth century cleared huge numbers of eastern chestnut and oak trees to make room for farms and towns. These trees were the passenger pigeon's main source of food. The birds were seen as a threat to crops, so people killed the birds. They were also hunted for food. All of these factors wiped out the passenger pigeon. The last one, which lived in the Cincinnati Zoological Garden, died on September 1, 1914.

Text Structure

Science articles often give important facts and figures. Underline the number that tells how many passenger pigeons a single flock once contained. In which part of the United States did passenger pigeons live?

_____

_____

Reading Strategy: Recognize Cause and Effect

Underline the sentence that tells why settlers killed the pigeons. What was the final effect on the pigeons?

_____

_____

_____

Comprehension Check

Circle the sentence that tells where the last passenger pigeon lived. What do you think might have been done to keep the passenger pigeon from becoming extinct?

_____

_____

The Carolina Parakeet

This colorful bird was the only parrot native to the eastern United States. It had green feathers with a yellow head and orange cheek patches and forehead. The largest Carolina parakeets were 33 centimeters (13 in.) long, including their tail feathers. They once lived throughout the Southeast, as far north as Virginia and as far west as Texas. Parrots are among the smartest of birds. However, farmers thought these fruit-eaters were pests. So they shot them from the skies. The Carolina parakeet became extinct in the 1920s. As a result, all that's left are stuffed examples of this bird in museums.

"Ivory-Billed Woodpeckers Make Noise"

Bird lovers were chirping back in April of 2005. Why? Scientists from Cornell University announced they'd rediscovered the ivory-billed woodpecker. The rare bird was thought to have been extinct since 1944. It was rediscovered at Cache River National Wildlife Refuge in eastern Arkansas.

In July, a small group of bird experts said that they weren't sure the ivory-billed woodpecker had really been rediscovered. They said a blurry videotape of the bird wasn't enough evidence. Researchers then decided to send them more proof. They shared a sound recording of the ivory-billed woodpecker's one-of-a-kind double-rap.

---

pests, small animals or insects that harm people or destroy things, especially crops or food supplies
Wildlife Refuge, protective environment for animals
one-of-a-kind, unique, or very special because there is nothing else like it

The unique sounds made believers out of the bird experts. "The thrilling new sound recordings provide clear and convincing evidence that the ivory-billed woodpecker is not extinct," said Richard Prum, a scientist from Yale University.

The ivorybill is the largest woodpecker in the United States. It has a wingspan of about 91 centimeters (3 ft.). The ivorybill began to disappear because loggers cut down forests across the Southeast between 1880 and the 1940s. Soon after the ivorybill was rediscovered, the U.S. government announced a $10 million plan to protect the rare bird.

Conservationists are trying to help the woodpecker by killing trees. Sound strange? The woodpecker feeds on beetle larvae found under the bark of dead trees. When the trees are killed, more beetles will likely be attracted to the trees. With more food for the woodpeckers, the species will have a better chance at recovering.

Only about thirty-five to fifty trees will be cut on four 4-acre sections of land. There are 2,000 to 2,800 trees on each section. In about two or three years, scientists hope the trees will have lots of beetles for the woodpeckers. Then the double-rap of the ivorybill will be a common sound.

---

larvae, young insects with soft, tube-shaped bodies, which will eventually become adult insects with wings

---

Choose one and complete:

1. Create a poster to show one of the birds featured in this article. Mention the reasons why it became rare or extinct.

2. Find out more about one of the extinct bird species. Write a one-page report based on your research.

3. Imagine you are a conservationist working to save the ivory-billed woodpecker. Write a letter to a friend to describe your work and explain why it is important.

Comprehension Check

Draw a box around the name of the expert who is quoted on this page. What did bird experts believe after they listened to the sound recording?

_____

_____

_____

Reading Strategy: Recognize Cause and Effect

List two effects of the rediscovery of the ivory-billed woodpeckers.

1. _____

2. _____

Text Structure

Circle the highlighted vocabulary word that appears on this page. Look at the definition. Then rewrite the definition in your own words.

_____

_____

_____

Retell It!

What are conservationists and the government doing to save ivory-billed woodpeckers?
Write a paragraph that explains their work.

_____

_____

_____

_____

_____

_____

_____

Reader's Response

Do you think settlers should have cut down trees in the 1800s? Why or why not?

_____

_____

_____

_____

Think About the Skill

How did recognizing cause and effect help you to better understand the article?

_____

_____

_____

_____

EDIT FOR MEANING

Read

You have read "Going, Going, Gone?" Now read one paragraph from it again.

The Dodo

The dodo was the first bird to be wiped out by people during modern times. Dodos were large, flightless birds. They were first seen around 1600 on Mauritius, an island in the Indian Ocean. Less than eighty years later, the dodo was extinct. The dodo's heavy, clumsy body made it an easy target for sailors, who hunted it for food. As forests were destroyed, so was the dodo's food supply. And the cats, rats, pigs, and other predators unleashed by sailors preyed on the dodos. Together, these factors led to the dodo's extinction.

Fix the Error

Each paragraph below contains the same information as the paragraph you just read. However, each paragraph contains one error. First, find the error. Then fix it by editing the sentence so the information is correct.

1. Find and fix the error.

The Dodo

In the ancient era, the first bird wiped out by people was the dodo. Dodos were first seen around 1600. They lived on Mauritius, an island in the Indian Ocean. Less than eighty years later, the dodo was extinct. They were large, flightless birds. Their heavy, clumsy bodies were easy targets for sailors who hunted the birds for food. Cats, rats, pigs, and other predators also ate the dodos. Plus, as forests were destroyed, so was the dodo's food supply. All these factors led to the dodo's extinction.

---

2. Find and fix the error.

The Dodo

The first bird wiped out by people in modern times was the dodo. Dodos were first seen around 1600 on Mauritius, an island in the Indian Ocean. Less than eighty years later, the dodo was gone. The dodo's sleek, thin body made it a difficult target for sailors, who hunted it for food. The cats, rats, pigs, and other predators the sailors unleashed preyed on dodos, too. People also destroyed forests, which provided food for the birds. Together, these factors led to the dodo's extinction.

FOCUS ON DETAILS

Word Search Puzzle

To complete this word search puzzle, you'll need to remember or search for details in the reading. Write the word from the text next to each clue. Then circle the answers in the puzzle below.

1. ☐ Lost forever: _____

2. ☐ Ivorybills are this type of bird: _____

3. ☐ Large, flightless bird that is now extinct: _____

4. ☐ Ivorybills eat this kind of larvae: _____

5. ☐ Carolina parakeets have feathers that are this color: _____

6. ☐ Researchers made this to prove ivorybills exist: _____

7. ☐ The one-of-a-kind tap of ivorybills: _____

8. ☐ A worker who cuts down trees: _____

9. ☐ A kind of pigeon that no longer exists: _____

10. ☐ Carolina parakeets once lived this far north: _____

Q	O	Z	D	O	U	B	L	E	R	A	P	X	L	N
C	F	P	W	S	O	M	Y	S	D	C	E	C	S	E
R	L	L	X	K	U	P	W	K	K	L	N	E	B	E
E	X	D	M	G	Z	A	T	H	U	Z	I	P	Q	X
C	X	Q	N	R	G	S	J	C	J	C	B	Y	V	T
O	X	M	B	E	B	S	B	O	E	E	W	Q	B	I
R	E	G	N	E	S	E	A	P	C	D	R	U	U	N
D	A	R	L	N	N	S	B	E	E	T	L	E	C	C
I	T	I	F	O	O	G	H	S	C	C	R	C	C	T
N	B	A	N	D	G	E	P	O	B	S	J	R	U	C
G	B	O	O	I	A	R	R	G	U	V	M	E	T	T
T	O	D	Q	F	G	D	E	H	B	B	Q	Z	S	H
K	L	G	F	P	I	R	E	R	L	O	G	G	E	R
X	V	I	R	G	I	N	I	A	C	T	E	T	Q	T
W	Y	X	G	U	W	O	O	D	P	E	C	K	E	R

1. Silently read the text below. Make sure you understand the point that each sentence is making.

2. Underline the word or words in each sentence that are most important. When you read, you should say these underlined words with expression.

3. Look again at the punctuation in the paragraphs. Remember that when a sentence ends in a period, you should read the words as a statement and take a breath before beginning a new sentence. When you see a comma, you should pause briefly. When you see an exclamation mark, you should sound excited. When you see a question mark, you should read as though you are asking a question.

4. Now read the paragraphs below out loud. Pay attention to the important words and punctuation as you read.

5. Write down any words that slowed you down. Practice saying these words out loud.

6. Read the text below out loud two more times. You may want to ask a friend or family member to listen to you and tell you their reactions to your reading.

"Ivory-Billed Woodpeckers Make Noise"

Bird lovers were chirping back in April of 2005. Why? Scientists from Cornell University announced they'd rediscovered the ivory-billed woodpecker. The rare bird was thought to have been extinct since 1944. It was rediscovered at Cache River National Wildlife Refuge in eastern Arkansas.

In July, a small group of bird experts said that they weren't sure the ivory-billed woodpecker had really been rediscovered. They said a blurry videotape of the bird wasn't enough evidence. Researchers then decided to send them more proof. They shared a sound recording of the ivory-billed woodpecker's one-of-a-kind double-rap.

Name _____ Date _____

How are courage and imagination linked?

READING 2: "Kids' Guernica"

SUMMARY *Use with textbook pages 284–287.*

This article tells about an international art project called Kids' Guernica. It was started by Yasuda Tadashi in Kyoto, Japan in 1995. Tadashi got his idea after seeing a famous mural by Pablo Picasso. The mural shows the bombing of Guernica, Spain. Tadashi contacted schools in areas affected by war. He encouraged the students to paint their own "Guernica" murals. These large paintings express the children's feelings toward war. They also show their hopes for a peaceful future. So far, more than 500 children from around the world have joined the Kids' Guernica project. The students say that they will continue making murals until there is world peace.

Visual Summary

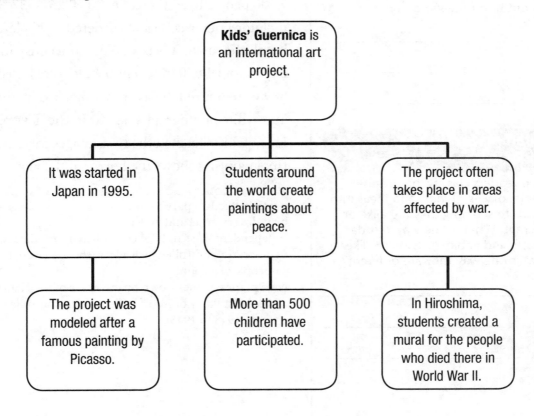

Kids' Guernica is an international art project.

It was started in Japan in 1995.

Students around the world create paintings about peace.

The project often takes place in areas affected by war.

The project was modeled after a famous painting by Picasso.

More than 500 children have participated.

In Hiroshima, students created a mural for the people who died there in World War II.

Use What You Know

List three reasons why someone might want to create a painting.

1. _____

2. _____

3. _____

Text Structure

A social studies text often has highlighted vocabulary words. **Mark the Text** Their definitions are at the bottom of the page. Circle the second highlighted word on this page. Look at its definition. Rewrite the sentence the term appears in without using the word.

_____

_____

_____

Reading Strategy: Classify

Good readers classify, or arrange, people, places, things, and ideas into groups to see how they are alike or different. What is one way Yasuda Tadashi and Pablo Picasso are alike? What is one way they are different?

_____

_____

_____

Kids' Guernica

In Kyoto, Japan, in 1995, Yasuda Tadashi started an international art project for peace. Its name was Kids' Guernica. Using the Internet, Tadashi organized schools around the world to participate. The goal was to have children in different parts of the world create peace paintings on huge canvases. The model for the project was one of the most famous paintings of the twentieth century.

Spanish artist Pablo Picasso (1881–1973) had painted *Guernica* in 1937 to protest the brutal bombing of a town in Northern Spain during the Spanish Civil War (1936–1939). Guernica had been an independent and democratic town. Around 7,000 people lived there. On April 26, 1937, Spanish dictator Francisco Franco ordered Nazi planes to bomb the town. It was 4:00 P.M. on a busy market day. About 1,650 innocent people were killed, and 889 were injured. Picasso was shocked by the black-and-white photographs he saw in the newspapers. He quickly sketched the first images for a mural. His final painting shows the horror and chaos of war.

participate, do a particular activity
brutal, very cruel and violent
independent, free and not controlled by another country
democratic, controlled by leaders who are elected by the people of a country
Nazi planes, planes flown by members of the National Socialist Party of Adolf Hitler, which controlled Germany from 1938 to 1945

Tadashi was inspired by Picasso's painting. Since 1995, he has organized children throughout the world to paint murals for peace that are the same size as the painting *Guernica*. The original painting is 3.5 × 7.8 meters (11.5 × 25.5 ft.). Children participate in workshops in their schools and create their own paintings.

Comprehension Check

Circle the year that Tadashi began the Kids' Guernica project. Who inspired him to get started?

_____

_____

_____

Reading Strategy: Classify

Draw a box around the kind of paintings students create for the project. Name one way their paintings are like Picasso's original painting.

_____

_____

_____

Comprehension Check

Underline the sentence that tells how children participate in the project. What is the size of the paintings they create?

_____

_____

_____

The Kids' Guernica project often takes place in areas that have been torn apart by war. Hiroshima, Japan, is one example. In 1945, the United States dropped an atomic bomb on Hiroshima, ending World War II. The city was completely destroyed. In 1999, forty-one students from four elementary schools in Hiroshima participated in the Kids' Guernica art project. These schools are all located in the area where the bomb exploded. The students created their mural in memory of the 140,000 people who died. Their mural also expresses hope for peace in the future.

The Kids' Guernica project has traveled all over the world. Children across the globe have used art to express their messages of peace. They have made murals in places such as Israel, Palestine, Afghanistan, Korea, and Kuwait. They have tried to spread peace on every continent. In 2004, children involved in the project made a mural for the United Nations building in Geneva, Switzerland. In 2005, the Kids' Guernica project celebrated its tenth anniversary with an art show in Bali, Indonesia. And in 2006 and 2007, participants in the project created murals in Kastelli, Crete, and Chios, Greece. So far, more than 500 children from schools in Cambodia, Sri Lanka, Chile, Nepal, India, Algeria, Germany, the United States, Australia, China, Canada, France, Italy, and other countries have participated.

The people involved in the Kids' Guernica project hope that their paintings will make the world a better place. They want to spread their powerful message around the globe. They say that the project will go on until there is world peace.

Choose one and complete:

1. Create your own drawing to celebrate peace. Write a paragraph to explain what the drawing honors or represents.

2. On an outline map of the world, highlight five countries where children have created murals as part of the Kids' Guernica project.

3. Imagine you are a TV reporter who is going to interview Yasuda Tadashi. Write a list of five questions to ask about the Kids' Guernica project.

Text Structure

Social studies includes not only history, but also geography, which is the study of places around the world. Circle the country where students created a mural in 2004. Where does the mural hang?

Mark the Text

_____

_____

_____

Comprehension Check

Draw a box around the year the project had its tenth anniversary. How did the people of Kids' Guernica celebrate?

Mark the Text

_____

_____

_____

Reading Strategy: Classify

How are the cities Kastelli and Chios connected to the Kids' Guernica project?

_____

_____

_____

Retell It!

Why did Pablo Picasso create his painting entitled *Guernica*? Explain the history of the town the painting was named after.

_____

_____

_____

_____

_____

_____

_____

Reader's Response

Do you think works of art can help bring about peace? Explain why or why not?

_____

_____

_____

_____

Think About the Skill

How did classifying help you better understand the article?

_____

_____

_____

_____

EDIT FOR MEANING

You have read "Kids' Guernica." Now read one paragraph from it again.

Kids' Guernica

In Kyoto, Japan, in 1995, Yasuda Tadashi started an international art project for peace. Its name was Kids' Guernica. Using the Internet, Tadashi organized schools around the world to participate. The goal was to have children in different parts of the world create peace paintings on huge canvases. The model for the project was one of the most famous paintings of the twentieth century.

Fix the Error

Each paragraph below contains the same information as the paragraph you just read. However, each paragraph contains one error. First, find the error. Then fix it by editing the sentence so the information is correct.

1. Find and fix the error.

Kids' Guernica

Kids' Guernica is a nationally based art project for peace that involves only the children of Japan. The project was started in 1995 by Yasuda Tadashi. Kids' Guernica was modeled after one of the most famous paintings of the twentieth century. Tadashi contacted schools to ask if their students could take part. His goal was to have children in different parts of the world create paintings for peace.

2. Find and fix the error.

Kids' Guernica

In Kyoto, Japan, Yasuda Tadashi started an international art project for peace. The project, which began in 1995, is called Kids' Guernica. Tadashi mailed schools around the world to bring them together. The goal was to have children in different parts of the world create paintings about war. The model for the project was one of the most famous paintings of the twentieth century.

Name _____ Date _____

FOCUS ON DETAILS

Crossword Puzzle

To complete this crossword puzzle, choose words from the box. Not all the words are answers to the puzzle. Use the clues to help you. You can also search for details in the reading to learn more about the words and clues below.

anniversary	project	murals	Hiroshima	memory
~~dictator~~	Guernica	sculptures	paintings	photographs
message	Cambodia	canvases	continent	world

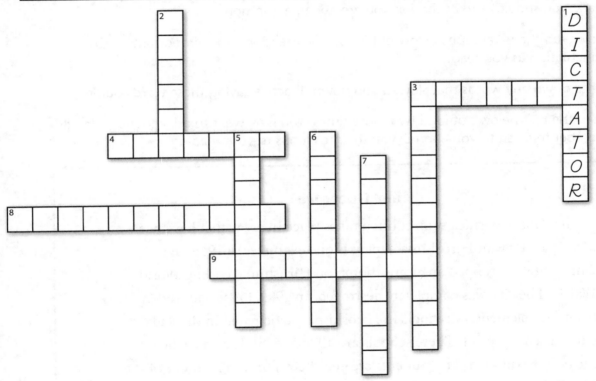

Across

3. Yasuda Tadashi started an art _____ for peace.

4. He wants to spread a powerful _____ around the globe.

8. They celebrated this with an art show in 2005.

9. During World War II, the United States dropped an atomic bomb on this Japanese city.

Down

1. Francisco Franco was this type of leader in Spain in the 1930s.

2. Children who participate in the project create these.

3. Black-and-white _____ of a bombing shocked Picasso.

5. The title of one of Picasso's famous paintings.

6. Children paint on huge _____ that are 3.5 × 7.8 meters.

7. Tadashi has tried to spread peace on every _____.

Unit 5 • Reading 2

1. Silently read the text below. Make sure you understand the point that each sentence is making.

2. Underline the word or words in each sentence that are most important. When you read, you should say these underlined words with expression.

3. Look again at the punctuation in the paragraphs. Remember that when a sentence ends in a period, you should read the words as a statement and take a breath before beginning a new sentence. When you see a comma, you should pause briefly. When you see an exclamation mark, you should sound excited. When you see a question mark, you should read as though you are asking a question.

4. Now read the paragraphs below out loud. Pay attention to the important words and punctuation as you read.

5. Write down any words that slowed you down. Practice saying these words out loud.

6. Read the text below out loud two more times. You may want to ask a friend or family member to listen to you and tell you their reactions to your reading.

Kids' Guernica

The Kids' Guernica project often takes place in areas that have been torn apart by war. Hiroshima, Japan, is one example. In 1945, the United States dropped an atomic bomb on Hiroshima, ending World War II. The city was completely destroyed. In 1999, forty-one students from four elementary schools in Hiroshima participated in the Kids' Guernica art project. These schools are all located in the area where the bomb exploded. The students created their mural in memory of the 140,000 people who died. Their mural also expresses hope for peace in the future.

Name _____ Date _____

How are courage and imagination linked?

READING 4: "A Tree Grows in Kenya: The Story of Wangari Maathai" / "How to Plant a Tree"

SUMMARY *Use with textbook pages 312–315.*

The first passage tells about a Kenyan environmentalist named Wangari Maathai. Maathai won the Nobel Peace Prize in 2004. She helped improve living conditions in Kenya and other parts of the world. Maathai believed that many of Kenya's problems were caused by the destruction of the natural environment. For example, cutting down forests caused poor soil conditions. It also caused shortages of clean water and firewood. In 1977, Maathai started the Green Belt Movement. Her goal was to encourage Kenya's farmers to plant trees throughout the country. Today, there are millions more trees thanks to Maathai's Green Belt Movement. The second passage, "How to Plant a Tree," gives step-by-step instructions for planting a tree.

Visual Summary

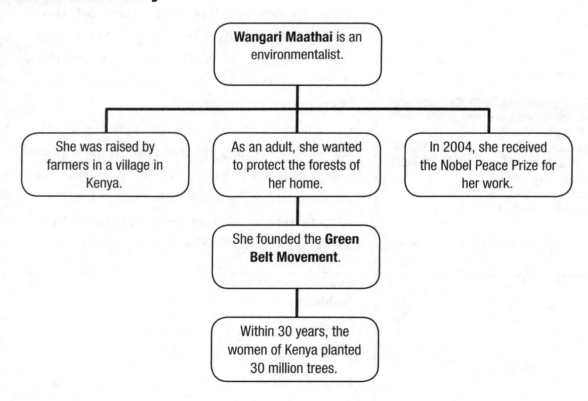

Use What You Know

List three things you know about trees.

1. _____

2. _____

3. _____

Text Structure

A science text often has highlighted vocabulary words. Their definitions are at the bottom of the page. Draw a box around the second highlighted word on this page. Look at its definition. Rewrite the sentence the word appears in without using the term.

Mark the Text

_____

_____

_____

Comprehension Check

Circle the year Wangari Maathai was born. What details about her childhood may have predicted her career as an environmentalist?

Mark the Text

_____

_____

A Tree Grows in Kenya: The Story of Wangari Maathai

In October 2004, Wangari Maathai (wan-GAH-ree mah-DHEYE), an environmentalist from Kenya, Africa, received an unexpected phone call. The person on the phone told her that she had won the Nobel Peace Prize. Each year, the Nobel committee chooses someone whose work for peace is judged to be the most important to the world. This was an incredible honor and an enormous surprise for Maathai. She was very excited. In an interview with *Time* magazine, she said, "I think what the Nobel committee is doing is going beyond war and looking at what humanity can do to prevent war. Sustainable management of our natural resources will promote peace." She was pleased that the judges had recognized the deep connection between environmentalism and peace. "If we conserved our resources better," she said, "fighting would not occur."

Maathai's love of the environment began when she was very young. She was born in the highland village of Nyeri in Kenya in 1940. As a child she enjoyed the lush, green forests around her. Her parents were farmers, so she grew up close to the natural world. In her Nobel prize speech, she said:

humanity, people in general
highland, mountain

I would visit a stream next to our home to fetch water for my mother. I would drink water straight from the stream. Playing among the arrowroot leaves, I tried in vain to pick up the strands of frogs' eggs, believing they were beads. But every time I put my little fingers under them they would break. Later, I saw thousands of tadpoles: black, energetic, and wriggling through the clear water against the background of the brown earth. This is the world I inherited from my parents.

Maathai was an excellent student. She won a scholarship to attend a college in the United States. She studied hard and received a degree in biology. Then she worked toward more advanced degrees at the University of Pittsburgh and University of Nairobi in Kenya. In 1971, she earned a doctoral degree. She was honored to be the first woman in East and Central Africa to earn such an advanced degree.

---

tadpoles, small creatures with long tails that live in water and grow into frogs or toads
inherited, received
scholarship, money given to help pay for a person's education

Text Structure

Science articles often include quotations. Draw a box around the quotation that appears on this page. Who is speaking? What is he or she talking about?

_____

_____

_____

Reading Strategy: Follow Steps in a Process

Steps in a process describe the steps in completing a task. In your own words, describe the steps Maathai took to get an education.

_____

_____

_____

Comprehension Check

Circle the year Maathai received a doctoral degree. How many other women in East and Central Africa had attained such an advanced degree?

_____

_____

_____

Comprehension Check

Underline the place where Maathai taught after she completed her education. Was she satisfied with this job? Why or why not?

Mark the Text

_____

_____

_____

Text Structure

Circle the first highlighted vocabulary word on this page. Look at the definition. Then use the word in a new sentence.

Mark the Text

_____

_____

_____

Reading Strategy: Follow Steps in a Process

What was the first step Maathai took to help save the forests of Africa? Why do you think this was the first step she chose to make?

_____

_____

_____

At first, Maathai taught at the University of Nairobi. Soon she wanted to do more than teach. While in the United States, she had been deeply impressed by the democratic freedom that people enjoyed. She wanted the Kenyan people to enjoy similar freedom and a better quality of life.

Maathai was concerned that the luxuriant forests of her childhood were rapidly disappearing because of excessive logging and other practices. She wanted the people of her village, especially the women, to have more of a voice in government. Maathai decided that it was time for a change.

It is said that "a journey of a thousand miles begins with a single step." Maathai took one step to change the world around her: She planted nine trees in her backyard. With this simple act, she planted the seed of her campaign to save the forests of Africa!

---

luxuriant, healthy, thick, and strong
excessive, much more than reasonable or necessary

In 1976, Maathai interviewed many farmers in the Kenyan countryside. Most of them were women, and they often had the same concerns. They needed more firewood, which was their main source of energy. They needed clean water for drinking, cooking, and bathing. They needed to be able to grow their own food. In addition, they needed to be able to make more money so that they could become self-sufficient.

Maathai knew that the destruction of the forests was at the root of these problems. She decided to put her knowledge and creativity to work. Trees were needed to stop soil erosion. They were also important sources of firewood for cooking. Why not encourage farmers in Kenya to plant as many trees as possible? This would be a simple way to improve the farmers' living conditions. And this method wouldn't require expensive tools or large sums of money.

self-sufficient, able to provide for themselves
erosion, destruction and wearing away because of wind and rain

Comprehension Check

Underline the sentence that tells the reason why farmers in Kenya wanted to make more money. List three other things the farmers said they needed.

1. _____

2. _____

3. _____

Text Structure

Circle the first highlighted word on this page. Look at its definition. Then rewrite the definition in your own words.

_____

_____

_____

Comprehension Check

Underline the sentence that tells the root of the farmers' problems. What solution did Maathai think of to solve it?

_____

_____

_____

In 1977, Maathai founded the Green Belt Movement. A greenbelt is a band of farmland or parks surrounding a village. Maathai hoped to see belts of green trees again throughout Kenya. The goals of the Green Belt Movement were to encourage Kenyan farmers to plant trees and to conserve the environment. This, in turn, would help farmers, and women in particular, to improve their living conditions.

At first, her idea wasn't very popular. As Maathai said, "It took me a lot of days and nights to convince people that women could improve their environment without much technology or . . . financial resources." Although it took a long time, the movement achieved its goal. Within thirty years, the women of Kenya had planted 30 million trees. The Green Belt Movement did other things to improve the quality of Kenyan life. Members also promoted better education and nutrition throughout the country.

---

financial resources, money or access to money

When Maathai started her campaign to plant trees, she was working at the grass-roots level. This means that she worked directly with the local people. Sometimes, she also worked directly with the government to bring about change. For example, in the 1980s, Kenyan President Daniel arap Moi planned to build a sixty-two-story skyscraper. This plan would have destroyed Uhuru Park, a beautiful park in Nairobi, the nation's capital. Maathai had visited Uhuru Park many times. It was one of the only green spaces available in the city for public use. Families often went there on weekends to relax, play, and enjoy time together. To save this precious green space, she led protests against the government. President Moi called her "a threat to the order and security of the country." Maathai was arrested by the police and treated badly, but she never gave up the fight. Because of her courage and persistence, she eventually succeeded in preserving the park.

skyscraper, very tall building
precious, valuable and important
persistence, determination

Comprehension Check

Circle the location of Uhuru Park. Why did Maathai want to protect the park?

Mark the Text

_____
_____
_____

Text Structure

Draw a box around the second highlighted vocabulary word on this page. Look at the definition. List one synonym for this word.

Mark the Text

_____
_____
_____

Reading Strategy: Follow Steps in a Process

What step did Maathai take to preserve Uhuru Park? What was the result of this action?

_____
_____
_____

Wangari Maathai strongly believes that solutions to most of the world's problems will come from the people themselves. She is now a national hero in Kenya. If young Kenyan girls are strong-willed and outspoken, people say they are "like Wangari." "Like Wangari" has become an expression of admiration and affection.

Today, Wangari Maathai and the members of the Green Belt Movement continue to plant trees throughout many countries in Africa, as well as in Haiti and the United States. They have educated thousands of people along the way. As the Nobel committee said, "Maathai is a strong voice speaking for the best forces in Africa to promote peace and good living conditions on the continent. She thinks globally and acts locally."

strong-willed, determined to achieve goals
outspoken, expressing opinions honestly and directly
admiration, approval and respect

How to Plant a Tree

What You Need

- Something to dig with, like a shovel or spade.
- A tree! You can buy a tree at a garden center. In some places, state or community foresters have trees that they'll give to anyone who wants to plant them. When you buy your tree, you'll notice that all of its roots are wrapped up with fabric in a little ball. This is called the rootball.
- A watering can and some water.

What To Do

1. First, choose a site. Pick a place that gets enough sun, where your tree will be happy. Don't plant close to power or telephone wires.
2. Dig a hole as deep as the rootball and three times as wide.
3. Unwrap the rootball and spread out the roots. If they're tangled up, straighten them out.
4. Put the tree in the hole. The soil should come up as high on the tree as it was before you got it. Usually this will be to the top of the rootball. Be sure that the tree is straight.
5. Fill in the space around the rootball gently but firmly with soil. Pack down the soil with your hands and feet. Be sure that there are no air pockets.
6. Make a little dam around the base of the tree about as wide as the hole. This will keep the water close to the tree.
7. After it's planted, your tree will be very thirsty, so give it lots of water.
8. If you need more help, call your local garden store or contact a community park or forest agency.

Some Tips to Keep in Mind

- If you want to plant your tree in a park or other public place, make sure you ask for permission. Some places may have rules about what kind of trees can be planted there.
- Your tree is just a baby, and like any baby, you need to take care of it. You should water it every week. Most trees need 7.5 to 11 liters (2–3 gal.) of water per week.

Comprehension Check

Underline the passage that explains where you can find a tree to plant. List the three things you need to plant a tree.

Mark the Text

1. _____

2. _____

3. _____

Reading Strategy: Follow Steps in a Process

Steps in a process describe the steps to completing a task. These steps are often listed in order from first to last. What is the last step to planting a tree? What is the first step?

1. _____

2. _____

Text Structure

Science articles often include tips to help you complete a task. Draw a box around the tips that appear on this page. How much water should you give a tree each week?

_____

Choose one and complete:

1. Draw a poster to encourage people to plant a tree. Explain why trees are important.
2. Create a time line that shows important dates in the life of Wangari Maathai.
3. Imagine you are presenting the Nobel Peace Prize to Wangari Maathai. Write a short speech to explain why she has been awarded the Nobel Peace Prize.

Retell It!

When Wangari Maathai interviewed the farmers of Kenya, what problems did they describe? What was her solution to these problems?

_____

_____

_____

_____

_____

_____

_____

Reader's Response

What do you most admire about Wangari Maathai?

_____

_____

_____

_____

Think About the Skill

How did following steps in a process help you better understand the article?

_____

_____

_____

_____

EDIT FOR MEANING

You have read "A Tree Grows in Kenya: The Story of Wangari Maathai." Now read one paragraph from it again.

A Tree Grows in Kenya: The Story of Wangari Maathai

At first, her idea wasn't very popular. As Maathai said, "It took me a lot of days and nights to convince people that women could improve their environment without much technology or . . . financial resources." Although it took a long time, the movement achieved its goal. Within thirty years, the women of Kenya had planted 30 million trees. The Green Belt Movement did other things to improve the quality of Kenyan life. Members also promoted better education and nutrition throughout the country.

Fix the Error

Each paragraph below contains the same information as the paragraph you just read. However, each paragraph contains one error. First, find the error. Then fix it by editing the sentence so the information is correct.

1. Find and fix the error.

A Tree Grows in Kenya: The Story of Wangari Maathai

At first, Maathai's idea wasn't very popular. She said, "It took no time at all to convince people that women could improve their environment." Eventually, the members of the movement managed to achieve their goal. They planted 30 million trees in 30 years' time. The Green Belt Movement did other things to improve the quality of life. Members also encouraged the people of Kenya to improve their nutrition and education.

---

2. Find and fix the error.

A Tree Grows in Kenya: The Story of Wangari Maathai

At first, Maathai's idea did not catch on. She said, "It took me a lot of days and nights to convince people that women could improve their environment." At the time, most believed the women would need a lot of money and technology to complete the task. Although it took a long time, the movement never achieved its goal. It took three decades, but they were able to plant millions and millions of trees. The Green Belt Movement did other things to improve the quality of Kenyan life. Members also promoted better education and nutrition throughout the country.

Name _____ Date _____

FOCUS ON DETAILS

To complete this mystery word puzzle, you'll need to remember or search for details in the reading. Use the clues to help you unscramble each of the words. Write the words in the boxes. The numbered letters will form the mystery word.

1. The capital city of Kenya

RONIBIA ⬜⬜⬜⬜⬜⬜⬜
　　　　　　1

2. The group Maathai formed is called the Green Belt _____.

TONVMEME ⬜⬜⬜⬜⬜⬜⬜⬜
　　　　　　2

3. As a child, she often saw thousands of these wriggling in a stream near her home.

SODLEPTA ⬜⬜⬜⬜⬜⬜⬜⬜
　　　　　　3

4. Maathai attended this in the United States.

CEGLELO ⬜⬜⬜⬜⬜⬜⬜
　　　　　7

5. She received her degree in this scientific field.

IYLOBGO ⬜⬜⬜⬜⬜⬜⬜
　　　　5

6. Kenyan forests were disappearing because of this and other practices.

GINGOLG ⬜⬜⬜⬜⬜⬜⬜
　　　　8

7. Planting trees does not require expensive _____ or large sums of money.

TOLSO ⬜⬜⬜⬜⬜
　　　4

8. A greenbelt is a band of _____ or parks around a village.

RAFMLDNA ⬜⬜⬜⬜⬜⬜⬜⬜

9. Maathai worked to do this and to protect Uhuru Park.

PEVSERRE ⬜⬜⬜⬜⬜⬜⬜⬜

10. The Nobel committee said Maathai ". . . thinks globally and acts _____."

LAOLYCL ⬜⬜⬜⬜⬜⬜⬜
　　　　6

When you buy a tree what are the roots wrapped up in?

⬜⬜⬜⬜⬜⬜⬜⬜
1　2　3　4　5　6　7　8

1. Silently read the text below. Make sure you understand the point that each sentence is making.

2. Underline the word or words in each sentence that are most important. When you read, you should say these underlined words with expression.

3. Look again at the punctuation in the paragraphs. Remember that when a sentence ends in a period, you should read the words as a statement and take a breath before beginning a new sentence. When you see a comma, you should pause briefly. When you see an exclamation mark, you should sound excited. When you see a question mark, you should read as though you are asking a question.

4. Now read the paragraphs below out loud. Pay attention to the important words and punctuation as you read.

5. Write down any words that slowed you down. Practice saying these words out loud.

6. Read the text below out loud two more times. You may want to ask a friend or family member to listen to you and tell you their reactions to your reading.

A Tree Grows in Kenya: The Story of Wangari Maathai

Maathai was concerned that the luxuriant forests of her childhood were rapidly disappearing because of excessive logging and other practices. She wanted the people of her village, especially the women, to have more of a voice in government. Maathai decided that it was time for a change.

It is said that "a journey of a thousand miles begins with a single step." Maathai took one step to change the world around her: She planted nine trees in her backyard. With this simple act, she planted the seed of her campaign to save the forests of Africa!

What is your vision of life in the future?

READING 1: "Life in the Future"

SUMMARY *Use with textbook pages 336–341.*

This passage predicts what our lives will be like in the future. A timeline shows predictions from the year 2012 to 2035. By 2100, the world's population will be 11 billion people. As the population grows, more and more people will live in tall buildings. The buildings will be like small cities. People will ride in cars that steer themselves and fly in hypersonic airplanes. The airplanes will travel five times faster than the speed of sound. People may also be able to fly with personal jetpacks. They may even live on Mars some day.

Visual Summary

Life in the Future		
How We Might Live	**How We Might Travel**	**How We Might Explore**
The population might reach 11 billion people by the year 2100.	Transportation might be much faster and greatly improved.	We might explore other planets.
We might live in tall apartment buildings that are like small cities.	Hypersonic planes might fly into outer space.	Astronauts could travel to Mars by 2020.
	Cars might steer themselves.	People might live on Mars one day.
	People might use personal flying machines called jetpacks.	

"Life in the Future"

Imagine traveling in a time machine into the future. What do you think life will be like? This timeline shows some predictions about the future.

2012 —	fire-fighting robots that can find and rescue people
2013 —	clothes that become cooler or warmer depending on the temperature
2014 —	robotic pets
2015 —	telephone calls between speakers of different languages translated in real time
2016 —	humans traveling to Mars
2020 —	cars that drive themselves on automated highways; artificial lungs, kidneys, and brain cells
2025 —	underground cities
2030 —	more robots than people in some countries
2035 —	fully functioning artificial eyes and legs; people cured of 98 percent of all cancers

cured, healed; restored to health

The Growing World

The world's population is growing very fast. In 1800, the population was about 1 billion. Now it is over 6.5 billion. One reason for this fast growth is that the birthrate is higher than the death rate. That is, there are more people being born than there are people dying. Also, medical advances and better living conditions help people live longer. Scientists predict that in the year 2100, the population will be 11 billion.

Future Cities

As the population grows, it will be necessary to rebuild existing cities and build new ones. Some apartment buildings will be like small cities. Architects have created a model for an apartment building in Tokyo. It will be 840 meters (2,750 ft.) high and will have 180 floors. A population of 60,000 will be able to live there. High-speed elevators will carry sixty people at a time. The building will have stores, restaurants, and cinemas. People won't ever have to leave!

---

elevators, machines in a building that carry people from one floor to another

Comprehension Check

Draw a box around the sentence that gives one reason why the world's population is growing very fast. How many people live in the world today?

_____

Text Structure

A science article often has headings. Headings can signal a change in the topic or a new direction. Circle the second heading on this page. What part of life in the future will this section describe?

_____

_____

_____

Reading Strategy: Take Notes

Underline details you might include in notes on the model of a future apartment building. How many floors does the model have?

_____

How is this apartment building of the future different from the ones we live in today?

_____

_____

_____

Hypersonic Planes

The National Aeronautics and Space Administration (NASA) is developing a hypersonic plane that will be able to fly at least five times faster than the speed of sound. It will be able to fly to outer space. NASA has produced a $230 million prototype plane, but it doesn't expect to use it for space travel until about 2020.

The X-43A prototype plane looks like a flying surfboard. It is thin and has a wingspan of 1.5 meters (5 ft.). It is 3.6 meters (12 ft.) long and weighs 1,270 kilograms (2,800 lbs.). This plane set a new world speed record by flying nearly ten times the speed of sound. A working version of the X-43A will be about 60 meters (200 ft.) long.

---

prototype, model

Name _____ Date _____

Cars of the Future

As more people own cars, the roads become more crowded. This causes more traffic jams and more accidents. The cost of traffic jams in the United States is about $78 billion per year—4.5 billion hours of travel time plus 26 billion liters (7 billion gal.) of fuel wasted sitting in traffic.

Car manufacturers are always looking for ways to make cars safer, faster, and more convenient. In the future, there may be automated highways. On these highways, cars will steer themselves. They will go faster and brake by themselves. Cars will have computers that pick up signals from magnets in the road.

---

steer, guide
magnets, pieces of iron that attract other pieces of iron

Comprehension Check

Circle the amount of money traffic jams cost the United States each year. What is one reason for the high number of accidents that also occur?

Mark the Text

_____

_____

_____

Text Structure

Draw a box around the first highlighted vocabulary term on this page. Look at its definition. Then use the term in a new sentence.

Mark the Text

_____

_____

_____

Reading Strategy: Take Notes

List three details you might include in notes about cars of the future.

1. _____

2. _____

3. _____

Jetpacks

People have always dreamed of flying. In the fifteenth century, the Italian artist Leonardo da Vinci drew many designs of flying machines. But a personal flying machine—or jetpack—has proved to be one of the most difficult inventions.

Jetpacks have appeared in such movies as *The Rocketeer*, *Spy Kids*, and *Minority Report*. A "rocket man" flew into the opening ceremony of the 1984 summer Olympics in Los Angeles. Jetpacks today can fly for only a short time. In the future, they will fly longer and go faster.

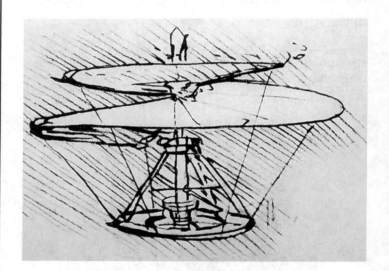

One of the most successful jetpacks is the Trek Aerospace Exoskeleton Flying Vehicle (EFV-4A). The EFV uses propellers to lift you off the ground. Once in the air, you can zip over treetops at 181 kilometers (113 mi.) per hour for 296 kilometers (184 mi.) before refueling.

New Frontiers

Throughout history, humans have loved to explore. Today, we have explored most of our planet. There are few new lands to explore, but there are new worlds, new planets, and new galaxies.

---

zip, move very fast
refueling, refilling with gasoline, oil, or some other fuel
galaxies, very large groups of stars

Comprehension Check

Underline the sentence that tells how one of the most successful jetpacks gets off the ground. What is this jetpack called?

_____

_____

Text Structure

Circle the first highlighted vocabulary word on this page. Look at the definition. List three synonyms for this word.

1. _____

2. _____

3. _____

Comprehension Check

Circle the sentence that tells how much of Earth we have explored. What new places are left to explore?

_____

_____

Comprehension Check

Draw a box around the kind of machine that has traveled to Mars. Have people ever made the trip?

Mark the Text

_____

Reading Strategy: Take Notes

List three details you would include in notes on the planet Mars.

1. _____

2. _____

3. _____

Text Structure

Circle the last highlighted vocabulary term on this page. Look at the definition. Rewrite the sentence the term appears in without using it.

Mark the Text

_____

_____

_____

In the future, perhaps we will colonize other planets. The most likely planet will be Mars. NASA scientists have already sent probes—spacecraft without people—to explore Mars. But when will people be able to go there? Astronauts could travel to Mars by about 2020. However, it will be a difficult task! It will take six months to reach the red planet. (It takes only three days to reach the moon.) And Mars is not a friendly environment. Mars probably once had liquid water, but now it is a cold, rocky desert. It has the largest volcano in the solar system and the deepest canyons. Dust storms can cover the whole planet. There is no breathable oxygen.

For people to live on Mars, the cities will have to be protected from the poisonous air. Giant domes will have to be built to control the atmosphere. All food will have to be grown inside the domed cities.

---

colonize, set up human communities
oxygen, a gas in the air that all plants and animals need in order to live
poisonous, deadly
domes, round roofs

Name _____ Date _____

Earth-Mars Comparison

	Earth	Mars
Average distance from sun	150 million kilometers (93 million mi.)	228 million kilometers (142 million mi.)
Length of year	365.25 days	687 Earth days
Length of day	23 hours, 56 minutes	24 hours, 37 minutes
Temperature	average 14°C (57°F)	average −63°C (−81°F)
Atmosphere	nitrogen, oxygen, argon, others	mostly carbon dioxide, some water vapor
Number of moons	1	2

Text Structure

A science article often has charts that compare information. Circle the two planets this chart compares. How many moons does each one have?

_____

_____

Reading Strategy: Take Notes

List three facts you would include in notes about the planet Earth.

1. _____

2. _____

3. _____

Comprehension Check

Draw boxes around the length of day on Earth and on Mars. How much longer is a day on Mars than on Earth?

_____

_____

Choose one and complete:

1. Draw a picture of a scene or activity that might take place in the future.

2. Create a brochure to encourage people to move into an apartment building in the future. Describe what it looks like and explain why people might want to live there.

3. Create a poster about Mars. Include important details about the planet.

Retell It!

How will transportation be different in the future? Describe what automobile and air travel might be like.

_____

_____

_____

_____

_____

_____

_____

Reader's Response

Do you think people will live on the planet Mars in the future? Explain why or why not.

_____

_____

_____

_____

Think About the Skill

How did taking notes help you better understand the article?

_____

_____

_____

_____

EDIT FOR MEANING

Read

You have read "Life in the Future." Now read one paragraph from it again.

The Growing World

The world's population is growing very fast. In 1800, the population was about 1 billion. Now it is over 6.5 billion. One reason for this fast growth is that the birthrate is higher than the death rate. That is, there are more people being born than there are people dying. Also, medical advances and better living conditions help people live longer. Scientists predict that in the year 2100, the population will be 11 billion.

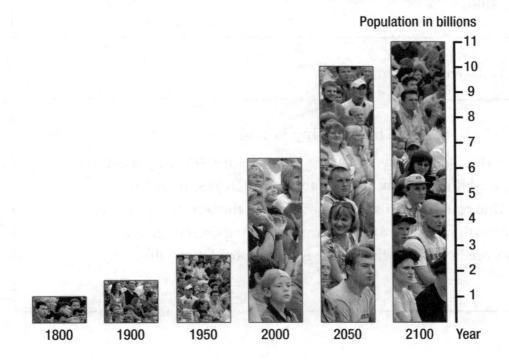

Population in billions

Fix the Error

Each paragraph below contains the same information as the paragraph you just read. However, each paragraph contains one error. First, find the error. Then fix it by editing the sentence so the information is correct.

1. Find and fix the error.

The Growing World

The world's population is steadily shrinking. In 1800, there were only about 1 billion people in the world. Now there are more than 6.5 billion. This is partly due to the fact that the birthrate is higher than the death rate. That means more people are being born than people are dying. This is because better living conditions and advances in medicine help people live longer. Scientists predict the population will be 11 billion by the year 2100.

2. Find and fix the error.

The Growing World

The world's population is growing very fast. In 1800, the population was about 1 billion. Today, that number has increased by about 5.5 billion. One reason for this fast growth is that the birthrate is higher than the death rate. There are fewer people being born than dying. Scientists predict that in about 100 years, the population will be 11 billion.

FOCUS ON DETAILS

Word Search Puzzle

To complete this word search puzzle, you'll need to remember or search for details in the reading. Write the word from the text next to each clue. Then circle the answers in the puzzle below.

1. ☐ By 2009, these machines might rescue people: _____

2. ☐ One day, people will colonize this planet: _____

3. ☐ One of the most successful jetpacks uses these to get off the

   ground: _____

4. ☐ In the future, cars might drive down this kind of highway: _____

5. ☐ The X-43A plane looks like this: _____

6. ☐ We still have new worlds, planets, and these to explore: _____

7. ☐ They could travel to Mars by about 2020: _____

8. ☐ These are deeper on Mars than any other planet in the

   solar system: _____

9. ☐ In the future, a car might use this to pick up signals from the

   road: _____

10. ☐ Giant domes will have to be built on Mars to control this: _____

```
R E G A L A X I E S R R U U E
O P Q N T C D J C U C B Y R P
B W R A T M A P E R M A R S N
O F P O E O M N S F C E C S A
T O D Q P G D I Y B A S E S T
S L G F L E R E R O O G G E M
I T I F C O L H S A N A C C O
N P R E O A T L R R S S P U S
D I S Q M N N S E D E T L E P
X V I R P I N I A R T E T S H
R L L X U U P W K K S N E B E
K X A U T O M A T E D I P T R
O X M B E B S E E L E W Q A E
G B O O R A R R E E V M E P R
I Y X G H A S T R O N A U T S
```

1. Silently read the text below. Make sure you understand the point that each sentence is making.

2. Underline the word or words in each sentence that are most important. When you read, you should say these underlined words with expression.

3. Look again at the punctuation in the paragraphs. Remember that when a sentence ends in a period, you should read the words as a statement and take a breath before beginning a new sentence. When you see a comma, you should pause briefly. When you see an exclamation mark, you should sound excited. When you see a question mark, you should read as though you are asking a question.

4. Now read the paragraphs below out loud. Pay attention to the important words and punctuation as you read.

5. Write down any words that slowed you down. Practice saying these words out loud.

6. Read the text below out loud two more times. You may want to ask a friend or family member to listen to you and tell you their reactions to your reading.

New Frontiers

In the future, perhaps we will colonize other planets. The most likely planet will be Mars. NASA scientists have already sent probes—spacecraft without people—to explore Mars. But when will people be able to go there? Astronauts could travel to Mars by about 2020. However, it will be a difficult task! It will take six months to reach the red planet. (It takes only three days to reach the moon.) And Mars is not a friendly environment. Mars probably once had liquid water, but now it is a cold, rocky desert. It has the largest volcano in the solar system and the deepest canyons. Dust storms can cover the whole planet. There is no breathable oxygen.

UNIT 6

What is your vision of life in the future?

READING 4: "Genetic Fingerprints"

SUMMARY *Use with textbook pages 380–383.*

This passage tells about DNA. DNA is a special code found in the cells of plants, animals, and people. Genes inside the DNA control the way we look and grow. No two people have the same DNA unless they are identical twins. Scientists use DNA to solve crimes. They can match the DNA found at a crime scene with the DNA of the criminals. DNA tests also help free innocent people from prison. The Innocence Project was started in 1992. It uses DNA testing to help prisoners prove their innocence. DNA has other uses, too. Scientists use it to identify food, bacteria, and objects from the past. DNA can also show if two people are from the same family.

Visual Summary

DNA (deoxyribonucleic acid)	
What It Is	**How It Is Used**
• It is a special code found in all living things.	• Sir Alec Jeffreys discovered how to make a DNA fingerprint.
• It is unique to each person.	• DNA fingerprints are used to identify people and solve crimes.
• Genes in DNA control the way we look and grow.	• DNA fingerprints are also used by chefs, medical researchers, and archaeologists.

Text Structure

A science text often has highlighted vocabulary words. Their definitions are at the bottom of the page. Circle the highlighted term on this page. Look at its definition. Rewrite the sentence the term appears in without using the word.

Mark the Text

_____

_____

_____

Reading Strategy:
Make Generalizations

A generalization is a statement that applies to most examples. It can be supported by facts. When you make a generalization, it helps you apply what you read to other situations. What generalization can you make about DNA and the human body?

_____

_____

_____

"Genetic Fingerprints"

Your fingerprints are unlike anyone else's. They have a pattern of ridges and whorls that is unique to you. The same is true of your DNA "fingerprints." You can't see them with the naked eye, but they have a pattern that is unique to you. Your DNA fingerprint exists in every cell of your body, and it is yours and yours alone.

The Wonders of DNA

Within the cells of your body, there is a chemical set of instructions, called DNA (deoxyribonucleic acid). These instructions tell a plant's or animal's body what it needs to grow and work.

You inherit about 80,000 genes from your parents. All 80,000 genes are present in each individual cell of your body. These genes contain the instructions that make you human.

Discovery of the DNA Fingerprint

In 1984, Sir Alec Jeffreys discovered how to make a DNA fingerprint. It happened by accident. He had been studying the differences in human DNA.

DNA is like a long, twisted ladder. The rungs of the ladder have a unique pattern of genes for each person. This unique arrangement of genes is what makes human beings different from one another.

Jeffreys took pieces of DNA. He marked them with a radioactive substance. Then he made images of these DNA fragments on X-ray film. When he developed the pictures, he was surprised at what he saw.

---

fragments, small pieces of something

Instead of a few isolated images . . . [he] saw long strings of images arranged in patterns. Dark bands—some thick, some thin—were stacked in patterns that looked a great deal like the bar codes found on products in the supermarkets (Fridell 18).

Here in visual form was a code that could be used to identify every living thing. This DNA "fingerprint" was a picture of a person's unique genetic code. Now scientists had solid evidence that they could use to uniquely identify people through their genes. Your DNA fingerprint, Alec Jeffreys said, "does not belong to anyone on the face of the planet who ever has been or ever will be."

DNA and Justice

Once DNA fingerprinting was discovered, it was used to identify people. Forensic scientists study crimes by looking at evidence. They use various scientific tests. Since the 1980s, they have used DNA fingerprints to investigate and solve crimes. They take a sample of blood, hair, or other body tissue found at the scene of a crime. This tissue contains DNA. The scientists check to see whether the DNA from a crime scene matches a sample of the suspect's DNA. This way they can figure out whether the suspect could have possibly committed a crime.

---

investigate, look into, research
tissue, material, such as skin and muscle
committed a crime, done something wrong or illegal

Comprehension Check

The quotation on this page explains what Jeffreys saw when he looked at the X-ray. Circle the passage that describes what DNA looks like. What do these patterns resemble?

_____

_____

_____

Text Structure

A science article often has headings. Headings can signal a change in the topic or a new direction. Draw a box around the heading on this page. How will this section most likely relate to what you have already read?

_____

_____

_____

Reading Strategy: Make Generalizations

False generalizations cannot be supported by facts. Is the statement *DNA fingerprints can be used to catch criminals* a true or false generalization? If it is true, underline one fact to support it.

_____

In recent years, many people have been released from prison after DNA tests proved that they were "wholly innocent." These people had not committed any crime at all.

In 1992, the Innocence Project was founded. It serves defendants who could be proved innocent through DNA testing. Since that time, innocence organizations have spread throughout the United States.

Law students at the Wisconsin Innocence Project investigate about twenty to thirty criminal cases at a time. In 2001, the project was responsible for the release of a Texas prisoner, Chris Ochoa. He was serving a life sentence for a 1988 murder. DNA tests on samples found on the victim proved that Ochoa did not commit the crime. He was innocent. Chris Ochoa had spent twelve years in prison for a crime he didn't commit. He is not alone. As of 2008, more than 200 people previously convicted of serious crimes have been found innocent because of DNA testing.

---

innocent, not guilty

DNA testing is now a very important tool in criminal investigation. It is going to be more important in the future. More forensic scientists are going to use DNA tests to help make sure the right people are punished for their crimes.

Other Uses of DNA Fingerprints

DNA is also being used in many other ways. For example, in India, chefs were having trouble identifying the type of rice they were cooking. Each type had to be soaked and cooked differently. So a rice producer used DNA fingerprinting to identify specific types. Now the chefs know how to cook each type correctly. Medical researchers have used DNA tests to identify and fight bacteria that cause food-related illnesses. DNA has also been used to investigate objects from the past. For instance, archaeologists have used DNA to help piece together the remains of the Dead Sea Scrolls. DNA fingerprinting has been used to identify family members who have been separated from one another because of wars or natural disasters. As DNA fingerprinting becomes increasingly popular, it will be used for many other purposes in the future.

bacteria, very small living things, some of which cause illness or disease
Dead Sea Scrolls, ancient texts, approximately 2,000 years old, discovered in caves near the Dead Sea

Comprehension Check

Underline the passage that tells how DNA fingerprinting helped chefs in India. What problem did they have?

_____

_____

_____

Text Structure

Circle the second highlighted vocabulary term on this page. Look at the definition. Then rewrite the definition in your own words.

_____

_____

_____

Reading Strategy: Make Generalizations

Is the statement *DNA fingerprinting can be used in many different fields* a true or false generalization? If it is true, underline one fact to support it. Explain why you think the generalization is true.

_____

_____

_____

_____

Choose one and complete:

1. Create a poster to show some of the ways DNA fingerprinting can be used.

2. Imagine you are a newspaper reporter. Write a short article on the Innocence Project to explain what they do and who they help.

3. Imagine you are making a documentary on DNA. What music would you use in the background? Describe your ideas.

Retell It!

How did Sir Alec Jeffreys discover how to make a DNA fingerprint? Describe all the steps in this process.

_____

_____

_____

_____

_____

_____

_____

Reader's Response

Do you think lawyers should use DNA evidence in criminal cases? Why or why not?

_____

_____

_____

_____

Think About the Skill

How did making generalizations help you better understand the article?

_____

_____

_____

_____

EDIT FOR MEANING

Read

You have read "Genetic Fingerprints." Now read one paragraph from it again.

DNA and Justice

Once DNA fingerprinting was discovered, it was used to identify people. Forensic scientists study crimes by looking at evidence. They use various scientific tests. Since the 1980s, they have used DNA fingerprints to investigate and solve crimes. They take a sample of blood, hair, or other body tissue found at the scene of a crime. This tissue contains DNA. The scientists check to see whether the DNA from a crime scene matches a sample of the suspect's DNA. This way they can figure out whether the suspect could have possibly committed a crime.

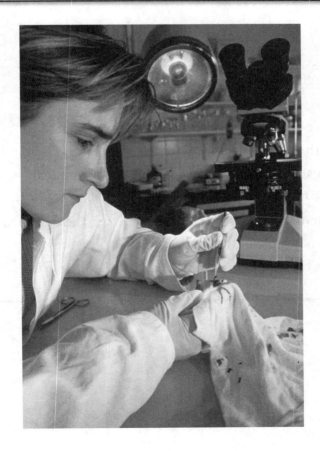

Fix the Error

Each paragraph below contains the same information as the paragraph you just read. However, each paragraph contains one error. First, find the error. Then fix it by editing the sentence so the information is correct.

1. Find and fix the error.

DNA and Justice

After DNA fingerprinting was discovered, it was soon used to identify people. Forensic scientists study crimes by looking at evidence and doing tests. Since the 1980s, they have used DNA fingerprints to investigate and solve crimes. They take a sample of evidence such as hair and blood found at the scene of a crime. These things contain a person's DNA. The scientists check to see whether the DNA from a crime scene matches a sample of the suspect's DNA. Unfortunately an exact DNA match does not prove anything at all.

---

2. Find and fix the error.

DNA and Justice

After it was discovered, DNA fingerprinting began to be used to identify people. Since the 1980s, forensic scientists have used DNA fingerprints to investigate and solve crimes. They take a sample of things such as blood or hair from the scene of a crime. These things contain DNA. The scientists do not check to see whether the DNA from a crime scene matches a sample of the suspect's DNA. This way they can figure out whether the suspect could have committed the crime.

Name _____ Date _____

Mystery Word Puzzle

To complete this mystery word puzzle, you'll need to remember or search for details in the reading. Use the clues to help you unscramble each of the words. Write the words in the boxes. The numbered letters will form the mystery word.

1. DNA can be used to identify people who are separated because of wars and

   natural _____.

   DEITSRASS   ☐☐☐☐☐☐☐☐☐
                3   8

2. You inherit about 80,000 of these from your parents.

   NEGSE   ☐☐☐☐☐
                11

3. Chefs in India have used DNA to identify this.

   CIRE   ☐☐☐☐
            4

4. DNA is a chemical set of instructions called deoxyribonucleic _____.

   DICA   ☐☐☐☐
          2

5. Since the 1980s, scientists have used DNA to _____ crimes.

   SVOLE   ☐☐☐☐☐
              10

6. Your DNA exists in every one of these in your body.

   LLSEC   ☐☐☐☐☐
          7

7. In 2001, the Innocence Project helped _____ a prisoner in Texas.

   SALREEE   ☐☐☐☐☐☐☐
                 6

8. Fingerprints are a pattern of ridges and these.

   LSWOHR   ☐☐☐☐☐☐
              5

9. This kind of scientist studies crimes by looking at evidence.

   ROCIFNES   ☐☐☐☐☐☐☐☐
                 1   9

   What kind of substance did Sir Alec Jeffreys use to mark DNA pieces?

   ☐☐☐☐☐☐☐☐☐☐☐
   1 2 3 4 5 6 7 8 9 10 11

Unit 6 • Reading 4   **145**

1. Silently read the text below. Make sure you understand the point that each sentence is making.

2. Underline the word or words in each sentence that are most important. When you read, you should say these underlined words with expression.

3. Look again at the punctuation in the paragraphs. Remember that when a sentence ends in a period, you should read the words as a statement and take a breath before beginning a new sentence. When you see a comma, you should pause briefly. When you see an exclamation mark, you should sound excited. When you see a question mark, you should read as though you are asking a question.

4. Now read the paragraphs below out loud. Pay attention to the important words and punctuation as you read.

5. Write down any words that slowed you down. Practice saying these words out loud.

6. Read the text below out loud two more times. You may want to ask a friend or family member to listen to you and tell you their reactions to your reading.

Other Uses of DNA Fingerprints

DNA is also being used in many other ways. For example, in India, chefs were having trouble identifying the type of rice they were cooking. Each type had to be soaked and cooked differently. So a rice producer used DNA fingerprinting to identify specific types. Now the chefs know how to cook each type correctly. Medical researchers have used DNA tests to identify and fight bacteria that cause food-related illnesses. DNA has also been used to investigate objects from the past. For instance, archaeologists have used DNA to help piece together the remains of the Dead Sea Scrolls. DNA fingerprinting has been used to identify family members who have been separated from one another because of wars or natural disasters. As DNA fingerprinting becomes increasingly popular, it will be used for many other purposes in the future.